Notebook

Robert Lowell
NOTEBOOK

FARRAR, STRAUS AND GIROUX
NEW YORK

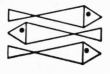

Copyright © 1967, 1968, 1969, 1970 by Robert Lowell
Third edition, revised and expanded, 1970
SBN 374.2.2325.4
All rights reserved
Library of Congress catalog card number: 69–13736
Published simultaneously in Canada
by Doubleday Canada Ltd., Toronto
Printed in the United States of America

Some of these poems were originally published in *New York
Review of Books,* and one in *New Republic,* to whose editors
grateful acknowledgment is made. "In the Cage" originally
appeared in *Lord Weary's Castle,* copyright 1944, 1946 by Robert
Lowell, and is used by permission of the publisher, Harcourt,
Brace and World, Inc.

Title page drawing by Francis Parker

for HARRIET
Even before you could speak,
without knowing, I loved you;
and for LIZZIE

Contents

Harriet, 1–4   *page* 21

Long Summer, 1–15   24

Outlaws: A Goodbye   32

For Mary McCarthy   33

Leaving   34

Searchings, 1–4   35

Les Mots   38

The Backward   39
     1 Dream of the Fair Women   39
     2 The Last Resort   39
     3 The Walk   40

Five Dreams   41
     1 The Old Order   41
     2 Agamemnon: A Dream   41
     3 The House in Argos   42
     4 The Next Dream   42
     5 Onion Skin   43

Through the Night, 1–7   44

The Muse   48
     1 Nantucket: 1935   48
     2 The Muses of George Grosz   48

Randall Jarrell: 1914–1965, 1–2   50

Munich 1938   *page* 52

October and November   53
   1 Che Guevara   53
   2 Caracas I   53
   3 The March I   54
   4 The March II   54
   5 Charles Russell Lowell: 1835–1864   55
   6 Caracas II   55

Autumn in the Abstract   57
   1 Alba   57
   2 In Sickness   57
   3 Deutschland über Alles   58
   4 End of the Saga   58

Symbols   60
   1 The Well   60
   2 Hell   60
   3 Rats   61
   4 In the Cage   61
   5 The River God   62
   6 The Leak   62

For Aunt Sarah   64

The Heavenly Rain   65

Charles River, 1–8   66

Thanksgiving   71
   1 Ulysses and Nausicaa   71
   2 Marching   71
   3 Romanoffs   72
   4 Two Farmers   72

Le Vieux Caton   74

Names   75
   1 Sir Thomas More   75
   2 Marcus Cato the Younger   75

3 Joinville and Louis IX	page 76
4 Alexander	76
5 Napoleon	77
6 Waterloo	77
Harvard, 1–4	79
Alcohol, 1–3	82
In the Forties, 1–3	84
Now	86
1 Candlelight Lunchdate	86
2 The Literary Life, a Scrapbook	86
Sleep, 1–3	88
To Margaret Fuller Drowned	90
Henry and Waldo	91
Dawn	92
Blizzard in Cambridge	93
Flight in the Rain	94
Christmas and New Year	95
1 Snake	95
2 Christmas Tree	95
3 The Dialogue	96
4 Playing Ball with the Critic	96
5 George H. and George E. Lewes	97
6 The Book of Wisdom	97
7 Trout	98
8 Descendant	98
9 Bird	99
10 Serpent	99
Mexico, 1–12	101
Canterbury	108
Killiecrankie	109
Midwinter	110
1 Friend across Central Park	110

11

2	*Another Friend*	*page* 110
3	*Judith*	111
4	*Seal of the Fair Sex*	111
5	*The Goldfish*	112
6	*La Lumière*	112
7	*Elisabeth Schwarzkopf in New York*	113
8	*Across the Yard: La Ignota*	113

School — 115
1	*For Peter Taylor*	115
2	*Randall Jarrell*	115

Lines From Israel — 117
1	*World War I, 1916*	117
2	*Sands of the Desert*	117
3	*Israel*	118

Writers — 119
1	*T. S. Eliot*	119
2	*Ezra Pound*	119
3	*Ford Madox Ford*	120
4	*To Allen Tate I*	120
5	*To Allen Tate II*	121
6	*William Carlos Williams*	121
7	*Robert Frost*	122

Those Older, 1–3 — 123

Death — 125

Ice on the Hudson, 1–2 — 126

Chairs — 128

My Death, 1–2 — 129

February and March — 131
1	*Cows*	131
2	*The Golden Middle*	131
3	*Father's Album*	132
4	*Vigil*	132
5	*Le Cygne*	133

6	Thirst	page 133
7	The Human Race	134
8	Helltime	134
9	Under the Screw	135
10	Oversleeping	135
11	In the Family	136
12	Left out of Vacation	136
13	Red and Black Brick Boston	137
14	Utopia for Racoons	137
15	Under the Dentist	138
16	Sense of Reality	138
17	Fame	139
18	Growing in Favor	139
19	Keepsakes: A Dead Letter	140
20	Last Summer	140
21	Cranach's Man-Hunt	141
22	Death and the Bridge	141
23	First Spring	142
24	Dear Sorrow	142
25	Rembrandt	143

Pastime, 1–2		144
April 8, 1968		146
1	Two Walls	146
2	Words of a Young Girl	146
3	Petit Bourgeois	147
Mania		148
1	1958	148
2	Heidegger	148
3	1968	149
Mania in Buenos Aires, 1962		150
April		151
1	Roulette	151
2	Europa	151

3 Redskin   page 152
4 Dalliance   152
5 Dialogue   153
6 The Misanthrope and the Painter   153
7 Even Such   154
8 The White Goddess   154
9 Topless   155
10 A Souvenir   155
11 Losers   156
12 Sappho   156
13 Good Losers   157
14 Antony   157
15 Aswan Dam   158
16 For Gallantry   158
17 A Moment   159
18 Wind   159

Abstractions   161

The Powerful   162
1 Allah   162
2 Attila   162
3 Clytemnestra   163
4 The Death of Count Roland   163
5 The Death of Alexander   164
6 Tamerlane Old   164
7 Bosworth Field   165
8 Lady Anne Boleyn   165
9 Charles V by Titian   166
10 The Army of the Duc de Nemours   166
11 Marlowe   167
12 Mary Stuart   167
13 Bishop Berkeley   168
14 Robespierre and Mozart as Stage   168
15 Saint-Just: 1767–1793   169

16 Coleridge and King Richard   *page* 169
17 Northwest Savage   170
18 Old Hickory   170
19 Abraham Lincoln   171
20 Sunrise   171
21 F. O. Matthiessen: 1902–1950   172
22 New Year's Eve 1968   172

1970 New Year   174

April's End   175
1 King David Senex   175
2 Night-Sweat   175
3 Caligula   176
4 Goiter Tests: Werner von Usslingen   176
5 Rush   177
6 Nostalgie de la Boue   177

Eloges to the Spirits   179
1 Revenants   179
2 Verdun   179
3 Hydrotherapy   180
4 Words for a Guinea-Pig   180

A Second Plunge, A Dream   182

For Norman Mailer   183

May   184
1 The Pacification of Columbia   184
2 Can a Plucked Bird Live?   184
3 Leader of the Left   185
4 The Restoration   185
5 Chienlit   186
6 The Ark   186
7 The New York Intellectual   187
8 In the American Grain   187
9 Dropout   188
10 The Dissenting Academy   188

11	The Doctor	*page* 189
12	West Side Sabbath	189
13	Revenant	190
14	New York	190
15	Open House	191
16	Sounds in the Night	191
17	Civilization	192
18	Publication Day	192
19	The Hunt	193
20	The Diamond Cutters	193
21	The Picture	194
22	Lunch Date	194
23	Piano Practice	195
24	Memorial Day	195

Robert Kennedy: 1925–1968 — 197

1	R.F.K.	197
2	Another Circle	197
3	Another June	198

To Summer — 199

1	The Worst Sinner	199
2	God of Our Fathers	199
3	White	200
4	Heaven	200
5	Quality I	201
6	Quality II	201
7	The House-Party	202
8	For Theodore Roethke 1908–1963	202
9	Professors of Tenure	203
10	Sacrificial Killing	203
11	For Eugene McCarthy	204
12	The Immortals	204
13	For Harpo Marx	205
14	Assassin!	205

15 *Milton in Separation*   *page* 206
16 *The Bond*   206
17 *Wall-Mirror*   207
18 *Stalin*   207

Eight Months Later   209
1 *Eight Months Later*   209
2 *Die Gold-Orangen*   209
3 *Volveran*   210

We Do What We Are   211
1 *The Nihilist as Hero*   211
2 *Grave Guild*   211
3 *Gap*   212
4 *In the Back Stacks*   212
5 *Reading Myself*   213

Rimbaud and Napoleon III   214

Circles   215
1 *Homing*   215
2 *The Hard Way*   215
3 *Das ewig Weibliche*   216
4 *Sound Mind, Sound Body*   216
5 *Penelope*   217
6 *Struggle of Non-Existence*   217
7 *The Spock etc. Sentences*   218
8 *The Good Life*   218
9 *Trunks*   219
10 *The Vague, The Vogue*   219
11 *For Archie Smith: 1917–1935*   220
12 *The Revolution*   220
13 *Youth*   221
14 *River Harbor*   221
15 *Shipwreck Party*   222
16 *Playing the* Archduke Trio   222
17 *High Blood*   223

17

18 *The Lost Tune*   *page* 223
19 *Death and the Maiden*   224
20 *Heat*   224

Grasshoppers   226

The Races   227
  1 *August*   227
  2 *Five-Hour Rally*   227
  3 *The Flaw*   228
  4 *Fear in Chicago*   228
  5 *'We Are Here to Preserve Disorder'*   229
  6 *After the Convention*   229
  7 *The Hospital*   230
  8 *Forethought*   230
  9 *November 6*   231
  10 *November 7: From the Painter's Loft*   231

Winter   233

Four Poems for Elizabeth Bishop   234
  1 *Water 1948*   234
  2 *Flying from Bangor to Rio 1957*   234
  3 *Letter with Poems for a Letter with Poems*   235
  4 *Calling 1970*   235

America from Oxford   237

Summer   238
  1 *These Winds*   238
  2 *Glass for Our Wedding Anniversary*   238
  3 *La Condition Humaine*   239
  4 *End of Camp Alamoosook*   239
  5 *Familiar Quotations*   240
  6 *Mink*   240
  7 *Cattle*   241
  8 *The Going Generation*   241
  9 *Bringing a Turtle Home*   242
  10 *Returning Turtle*   242

11 *The Stump and Green Shoots* *page* 243

12 *Christians* 243

13 *Nesting* 244

14 *No Hearing* 244

15 *Castine Harbor* 245

16 *Castine 1860* 245

17 *Joy* 246

18 *Nature* 246

19 *Growth* 247

20 *The Graduate* 247

21 *Outlivers* 248

22 *My Heavenly Shiner* 248

23 *It Did* 249

24 *Seals* 249

Father and Sons 251

1 *Michael Tate:* August 1967–July 1968 251

2 *Letter from Allen Tate* 251

The End 253

1 Dies Irae, *A Hope* 253

2 *On the Border* 253

For John Berryman 255

Closing 256

1 *Close the Book* 256

2 *Out of the Picture* 256

Half a Century Gone, 1–5 258

Obit 261

Afterthought 262

Note to the New Edition 264

Dates 265

Notebook

Harriet

1

Half a year, then a year and a half, then
ten and a half—the pathos of a child's fractions, turn-
ing up each summer. God a seaslug, God a queen
with forty servants, God . . . she gave up—things whirl
in the chainsaw bite of whatever squares
the universe by name and number. For
the hundredth time, I slice through fog, and round
the village with my headlights on the ground,
as if I were the first philosopher,
as if I were trying to pick up a car
key . . . It can't be here, and so it must be there
behind the next crook in the road or growth
of fog—there blinded by our feeble beams,
a face, clock-white, still friendly to the earth.

2

A repeating fly, blueblack, thumbthick—so gross,
it seems apocalyptic in our house—
whams back and forth across the nursery bed
manned by a madhouse of stuffed animals,
not one a fighter. It is like a plane
gunning potato bugs or Arabs on the screen—
one of the mighty . . . one of the helpless. It
bumbles and bumps its brow on this and that,
making a short, unhealthy life the shorter.
I kill it, and another instant's added
to the horrifying mortmain of

ephemera: keys, drift, sea-urchin shells,
packratted off with joy, the dead fly swept
under the carpet, wrinkling to fulfilment.

3

An unaccustomed ripeness in the wood;
move but an inch and moldy splinters fall
in sawdust from the aluminum-paint wall,
once loud and fresh, now aged to weathered wood.
Squalls of the seagull's exaggerated outcry,
dimmed out by fog . . . Peace, peace. All day the words
hid rusty fish-hooks. Now, heart's-ease and wormwood,
we rest from all discussion, drinking, smoking,
pills for high blood, three pairs of glasses—soaking
in the sweat of our hard-earned supremacy,
offering a child our leathery love. We're fifty,
and free! Young, tottering on the dizzying brink
of discretion once, we wanted nothing,
but to be old, do nothing, type and think.

4

To summer on skidding summer, the rude spring rain
hurries the ambitious, flowers and youth;
the crackling flash-tone's held an hour, then we
too follow nature, imperceptibly
change from mouse-brown to the white lion's mane,
to thin white, to the freckled, knuckled skull,
bronzed by decay, by many, many suns . . .
The child of ten, three quarters animal,
three years from Juliet, half Juliet,
already ripens for the night on stage—
beautiful petals, what shall I hope for,

knowing one choice not two is all you're given,
health beyond the measure, dangerous
to yourself, more dangerous to others?

Long Summer

1

At dawn, the crisp goodbye of friends; at night,
enemies reunited, who tread, unmoving,
like circus poodles dancing on a ball—
something inhuman always rising on us,
punching you with embraces, holding out
a hesitant hand, unbending as a broom;
heaping the bright logs brighter, till we sweat
and shine as if anointed with hot oil:
straight alcohol, bright drops, dime-size and silver. . . .
Each day more poignantly resolved to stay,
each day more brutal, oracular and rooted,
dehydrated, and smiling in the fire,
unbandaging his tender, blood-baked foot,
hurt when he kicked aside the last dead bottle.

2

Humble in victory, chivalrous in defeat,
almost, almost. . . . I bow and watch the ashes
blush, crash, reflect: an age less privileged,
burdened with its nobles, serfs and Faith.
Possessors. The fires men build live after them,
this night, this night, I elfin, I stonefoot,
walking the wildfire wildrose of those lawns,
filling this cottage window with the same
alluring emptiness, hearing the simmer
of the moon's mildew on the same pile of shells,
fruits of the banquet . . . boiled a brittle lobster-

shell-red, the hollow foreclaw, cracked, sucked dry,
flung on the ash-heap of a soggy carton—
two burnt-out, pinhead, black and popping eyes.

3

Months of it, and the inarticulate mist so thick
we turned invisible to one another
across the room; the floor, aslant, shot hulling
through thunderheads, gun-cotton dipped in pitch,
Salmon-glow as the early lighted moon,
snuffed by the malodorous and frosted murk—
not now! Earth's solid and the sky is light,
yet even on the steadiest day, dead noon,
the sun stockstill like Joshua's in midfield,
I have to brace my hand against a wall
to keep myself from swaying—swaying wall,
straitjacket, hypodermic, helmeted
doctors, one crowd, white-smocked, in panic, hit,
stop, bury the runner on the cleated field.

4

Here nature seldom feels the hand of man,
our alders skirmish. I flame for the one friend—
is it always the same child or animal
impregnable in shell or coat of thorns,
only kept standing by a hundred scared habits—
turtle the deft hand tips on its back with a stick?
I think of all the ill I do and will;
love hits like the polio of better days;
I always went too far. A day, that's summer;
whitecaps for acres strew the muddy swell.
I stand between tides; quickly bit by bit

the old crap and white plastic jugs lodge on the shore,
the ocean draws out the river to no end:
most things worth doing are worth doing badly.

5

The vaporish closeness of this two-month fog;
thirty-five summers back, the brightest summer:
the Dealer's Choice, the housebound girls, the fog;
fog lifting. Then, as now, the after curfew
boom of an unknown nightbird, local hemlock
gone black as Roman cypress, the barn-garage
below the tilted Dipper lighthouse-white,
a single misanthropic frog complaining
from the water hazard on the shortest hole;
till morning! Short dreams, short shrift—one second,
    bright
as burning shavings, scattered bait and ptomaine
caught by the gulls with groans like straining rope;
windjammer pilgrims cowled in yellow hoods,
making for harbor in their yellow bus.

6

The Romantic that springs, springs not in vain
in Don Giovanni's farcical, brute leaps . . .
O my repose, the goat's diminishing day.
Once in New Orleans when the ceiling fan
wrestled the moisture, and one pajama leg
hung out of reach, caught on a leather blade—
our generation bred to drink the ocean
in the all-possible before Repeal;
all girls then under twenty, and the boys
unearthly with the white blond hair of girls,

crawling the swimming pool's robin's-egg sky;
safe, and in reach. The fall warms vine and wire,
the ant's cool, amber, hyperthyroid eye,
grapes tanning on these tried entanglements.

7

Shake of the electric fan about our village;
oil truck, refrigerator, or just man,
nightly reloading of the village flesh—
there are worse things than marriage. Men find dates
whenever summer is on, these nights of the swallow
clashing in heat, storm-signal to stay home.
On Court Street, Dyer Lane, School, Green and Main,
the moon-blanched blacktop fusses like a bosom,
dropping through shade-trees to the shadeless haven—
woman's as white as ever. One only knows
mothers, the sweatshirt gorged with tennis balls,
still air expiring from the lavish arc—
we too wore armor, strode riveted in cloth,
stiff as the broken clamshell labeled man.

8

They come, each year more gallant, playing chicken,
then braking to a standstill for a girl;
soft bullets hitting bottles, spars and gulls,
echo and ricochet across the bay—
hardy perennials. Kneedeep in the cowpond,
far from this cockfight, cattle stop and watch us,
then, having had their fill, go back to lapping
soiled water indistinguishable from heaven.
The cattle get through living, but to *live*:
Kokoschka at eighty, saying, 'If you last,

you'll see your reputation die three times,
and even three cultures; young girls are always here.'
They *were* there . . . two fray-winged dragonflies,
clinging to a thistle, too clean to mate.

9

The shore is pebbled with eroding brick,
seaweed in grizzled furrows—a surf-cast away,
a converted brickyard dormitory; higher,
the blacktop; higher yet, a fish-hawk's nest,
a bungalow, view-hung and staring, with wash
and picture-window—here, like offshoots that
have taken root. Grass shooting overnight,
sticks of dead rotten wood in drifts, the fish
with missing eyes, or heel-print on the belly,
or a gash in the back from a stray hook;
the lawns, the paths, the harbor—stitched with motors,
yawl-engine, outboard, power mower, plowing
the mangle and mash of the monotonous frontier,
bottles of dirt and lighted gasoline.

10

Two in the afternoon. The restlessness.
Greek Islands. Maine. I have counted the catalogue
of ships down half its length: the blistered canvas,
the metal bowsprits, once pricking up above
the Asian outworks like a wedge of geese,
the migrant yachtsmen, and the fleet in irons. . . .
The iron bell is rocking like a baby,
the high tide's turning on its back exhausted,
the colored, dreaming, silken spinnakers
reach through the patches in the island pine,

as if vegetating millennia of lizards fed
on fern and cropped the treetops . . . or nation of gazelles,
straw-chewers in the African siesta. . . .
I never thought scorn of things; struck fear in no man.

11

Up north here, in my own country, and free—
look on it with a jaundiced eye, you'll see
the manhood of the sallowing south, *noblesse
oblige* turned redneck, and the fellaheen;
yet sometimes the Nile is wet; life's lived as painted:
those couples, one in love and profit, swaying
their children and their slaves the height of children,
supple and gentle as giraffes or newts;
the waist still willowy, and the paint still fresh;
decorum without hardness; no harness on
the woman, and no armor on the husband,
the red clay Master with his feet of clay,
catwalking lightly through his conquests, leaving
one model, dynasties of faithless copies.

12

Both my legs hinged on the foreshortened bathtub,
small enough to have been a traveler's . . .
sun baking a bright swath of balsam needles,
soft yellow hurts; and yet the scene confines;
sun falls on so many, many other things:
someone, Custer, leaping with his wind-gold scalplock,
a furlong or less from the old-style battle,
Sitting Bull's, who sent our hundreds under
in the Indian Summer—Oh that wizened balsam,
this sunlit window, the sea-haze of gauze blue

distance plighting the tree-lip of land to islands—
wives split between a playboy and a drudge.
Who can help us from our nothing to the all,
we aging downstream faster than a scepter can check?

13

Everyone now is crowding everyone
to put off leaving till the Indian Summer;
and why? Because everyone will be gone—
we too, dull drops in the decamping mass,
one in a million buying solitude. . . .
We asked to linger on past fall in Eden;
there must be good in man. Death bears us. Life
keeps our respect by keeping at a distance—
death we've never outdistanced as the Apostle boasted . . .
stream of heady, terrified poured stone,
suburban highway, rural superhighway,
sprig of skunkweed, mast of scrub . . . the rich poor—
we are loved by being distant; love-longing
mists the windshield, soothes the eye with milk.

14

Mischievous fish-shapes without scale or eye
swimming your leaf-green teagown, maternal, autumnal,
swirling six inches past the three-inch heel,
collapsing on us like a parachute,
in a spate of controversial spatter . . . then
exhaustion. We hunger for the ancient fruit,
marriage with its naked artifice;
two practiced animals, close to widower
and widow, greedily bending forward
for the first handgrasp of vermilion leaves,

clinging like bloodclots to the smitten branch—
summer afield and whirling to the tropics,
to the dogdays and dustbowl—men, like ears of corn,
fibrous growths . . . green, sweet, golden, black.

15

Iced over soon; it's nothing; we're used to sickness;
too little perspiration in the bucket—
in the beginning, polio once a summer. Not that;
each day now the cork more sweetly leaves the bottle,
except a sudden falseness in the breath,
passive participation, dogged sloth,
angrily skirting greener ice, the naught
no longer asset or advantage. Sooner
or later, and the chalk wears out the smile,
this life too long for comfort and too brief
for perfection—Cro-Magnon, dinosaur—
the neverness of meeting nightly like surgeons'
apprentices studying their own skeletons,
old friends and mammoth flesh preserved in ice.

Outlaws: A Goodbye

(TO SIDNEY NOLAN)

Always that pale, late glaze of afternoon,
and the chopped French conscripts of some war
in stumps and berets playing *boule* at Pau—
what's more honorable than innocent foemen
who risk life and honor to kill the innocent?
Ned Kelly walked mugged and bloodied to Barracks Hall,
'Our blood spoiled the lustre of the paint on the gatepost . . . .
While the outlaw reigns, your pockets swell;
'tis double pay and country girls.' You've gone.
Two rootstumps sit upright like skeletons of geese
sailing the upstream current on a saddle of drift;
five crows light up, the wing-noise panting hounds . . . .
Old Hand, we sometimes feel frenzies to seize the floor;
truth, alas, is the father of knowing something.

For Mary McCarthy

Your eight-inch, star-blue, softwood floorboard, your house
sawn for some deadport Revolutionary squire. . . .
A white horse doing small-point, flitching flies and smiling,
Dark Age luminary and Irish hothead,
the weathered yeoman loveliness of a duchess,
pale Diana, and rash to awkwardness. . . .
Whose will-shot arrows sing cleaner through the pelt?
You might say *will*, and not intelligence?
Others go on thinking it mind, mind, mind,
foundation on foundation, rococo stung,
stung repeatedly, by the battering ram's brass head of brass. . . .
I slip from wonder into bluster; you align
your lines more freely, ninety percent on target—
we can only meet in the bare air.

Leaving

This halfway madness, injection or infection,
her each syllable and humor renewed, rechewed,
her discards sacred, the hairpin, light hair on the blanket,
loved person never in the clear with conscience—
I hang by a kitetail. In the village, the lovers
stop for its unreliable clock and bells,
kept straight by intuitive tact and considered malice.
We leave, blood raps the leather on the ball of my foot;
I hear the young voice of another age and habit,
walking to London or Paris, 'You little knew
I could hardly put one foot before the other.'
He went on to be Lord Mayor or guillotined,
passed many varieties of untried being. . . .
The New York streets drink changes like a landscape.

Searchings

1

I return then, but not to what I wanted—
a dull invulnerability to failure,
blood shooting through the fingertips of ivy,
hair and blown leaf bosom, the arrogant
tanned brunt behind your snow-starched shirt. . . . The white
bluffs rise above the old rock piers, now wrecked
beyond insuring by two hurricanes—
a boy would mount those scattered blocks, and leave
the sultry Sunday seaside crowds behind,
seeking landsend, his light fishing rod,
duller and dimmer than a penciled eyebrow—
the boy, held over in the hollow classroom,
sanding down *RTSL*, his four initials, slashed
like a dirty word across the bare, blond desk.

2

I like the trees, because I can never be at their eye-level;
not even when the stiff sash of the New Hampshire farmhouse
slammed, as it always did, toward morning rise:
I dreaming I was sailing a very small sailboat,
with my mother one-eighth Jewish, and *her* mother two-
    eighths,
down the Hudson, twice as wide as it is, wide as the Mississippi,
sliding under the pylons of the George Washington Bridge,
childhood's twice-as-wide and twice-as-high,
lacework groins as tall as twenty trees—
landing in the coalsmoke and roses of

this river bar. . . . I am refreshed by the subway stop breath
of the black iron arbor. My knee-joints are melting—
O why was I born of woman? Never to reach their eye-level,
seeing the women's mouths while my date delays in the john.

3

There was no break-through, and no knowledge—just
the thrilling, chilling silver of your laugh,
hysterical digging of the accursed spur,
Amazon, who saw me, cool and pop-eyed,
ageless and holding back your war-whoop—no chicken,
still game for swimming bare-ass with the boys.
Where are the boys who fell in the hole to China?
The mongrel's chain rattles, but the post stands fixed.
We have only fallen in wars, our unnegotiable
flag still floats the seven seas like a bond. . . .
Man is ninety-nine hundredths water, bred of water,
water fowl and water weed and whale,
water to water to water to water to water. . . .
Best to pass through this war, hope, death . . . dead drunk.

4

Almost innumerable the ties withheld;
nothing straitens you though, as with glassy eye
you weigh the frenetic goldfinch slung about
your lighthouse promontory, flights an inch
from combustion and the drab of ash—
a thousand summers . . . I would not count them; twenty
years back, your body was much the same as today,
dressed in a boy's bone-muscle, grit and curling lip . . .
even the treasonable bulge behind your fabric—
pile earth on earth, you cannot bury it!

Never revealed to me. I trust in your youth then;
youth keeps the foamrubber waterfall
from falling, makes the falling flesh stand firm
marble, pear-pointing to eternity.

Les Mots

Two years above us, but below our height,
Leon Straus, ninthgrade fullback, his red shirt
I fantasied in the house across the street—
passion that put a motor in my heart. . . .
In love the choices are few and violent,
we wanted what no marriage safely scorns:
breasts stacked like a hawknest in her yellow shirt;
not the cloister, the Bible had lost its voice;
nor adultery, each withdrawal is the deathshot;
nor common sleep that hands us back to life—
we knew better places to cast our saffron sperm. . . .
Is it refusal of error breaks a life—
the supreme artist, Flaubert, was a boy before
the mania for phrases dried his heart.

The Backward

1 The Dream of Fair Women

Those maidens' high waists, languorous steel and wedding
   cake,
fell, as waists would, white, white bust to white heel—
these once, the new wave; mostly they were many,
and would not let us speak. Girl-aunts, our sisters—
pace, pace: loss of innocence
never threw them; when we are impotent,
they are faithful. They'll keep us to the road
from chapel to graveyard. When they smooth the dead cheek,
it bleeds; the birch tree turns to a telephone pole,
knobs and tears and maidenhair—their plots
want no man's seeding; best of all they live.
Ten hours of this are like ten years back home,
when hurting others was as necessary as breathing,
hurting myself more necessary than breathing.

2 The Last Resort

This sunrise, this *cri de coeur*, my swat at age,
the ten or twelve years my coeval gives himself
in the new bubble of divorce . . . ten or twelve years.
Old people in thirty canebacks view Vermont,
a golf course, and the everlasting hills.
In quantity or inns, they terrify;
their club is open to all who treasured health.
Now we and they are almost one soul in nothing.
No coldness! Dew soaks the golf-brogue, they move their
   cars,

burn the fast road toward Boston to the world—
an old house sunk and glum, a smell of turtles;
my grandparents young; their portrait fades to carbon.
Didn't she love him when she picked his clothes?
That marriage was rainy, youth that gives no youth.

3 *The Walk*

Those days no *casus belli* on earth to fight,
except the familial, hidden fundamental—
walks that married us to ourselves or a girl,
tomorrow that promised courage to die content.
The willow stump puts out thin wands in leaf,
a green and fleeting taste of unmerited joy,
the first garden, each morning, the first man,
and birds were laughing in the distant trees,
the Manichaean South of wars and orchards.
I am a free man, no one serves me; earth,
the great beast, clanks its chain of vertebrae. . . .
A true conservative hates change per se.
At the end of the long walk, your old dog dies of joy
whenever you sit down, a poor man at a fire.

Five Dreams

1 The Old Order

Eyes shut, I see them focus through my eyelids:
first a bull's-head, Cretan black-bronze, high cheekbone
still brave with gilt—too military; I see
a girl's Bacchanalia with a wicker cow's-head;
she died of sleeping pills, but there's a tongue
of silverfoil still sticks in the wicker mouth;
now it's a horse's-head; this is better, it's nervous,
its eyes are string-shot like the bull's; but now,
my bestiary is interrupted: the man,
the beauty in checker trousers, strides the schoolroom;
he is eloquently angry, confiscates the ink-pots;
I wouldn't try this, but perhaps he did right—
a groom works the gatelock to the freestone graveyard—
old law and order that locked at the tap of a glove.

2 Agamemnon: A Dream

As I sleep, their saga comes out clarified:
why for three weeks mother toured the countryside,
buying up earthenware, big pots and urns,
Goliath's potsherds, such as the savage first
archaeologist broke on the first dig . . . not *our* art—
common the clay, kingly the workmanship.
As I sleep, streams of butane leak from my lighter;
for three weeks mother's foreign in-law kept carving
his chess-sets, leaf green, leaf red, as tall as urns,
modern Viking design for tribal Argos.
A king trips on his pawns. Suddenly, I see

father's eyes cross and bubble—a whiff of butane,
the muscle of a spitted ox bubbling by the urn. . . .
Can I call the police against my own family?

3 The House in Argos

O *Christmas tree, how green thy branches*—the features
could only be the most conventional,
the hardwood smiles, the Trojan rug's abstraction,
the firelight dancing to the Christmas candles,
the unusual offspring with his usual scowl,
naming all fifty states of Paradise,
with a red, blue, yellow pencil, while his mother,
seasick with marital unhappiness—
she has become the eye of heaven, she hates
her husband swimming like vagueness, like a porpoise,
on the imperial scarlet of the rug. . . .
His corpse in the candles is a red gold lion,
his head is like the rich collection-plate,
singing, 'O Christmas tree, how green thy branches. . . .'

4 The Next Dream

'After my marriage, I found myself in constant
companionship with this almost stranger I found
neither agreeable, interesting, nor admirable,
though he was always kind and irresponsible.
The first years after our first child was born,
the daddy was out at sea; that helped, I could bask
on the couch and stimulation of my dreams,
but the courtship was too swift, the disembarkment
dangerously abrupt. I was animal,
healthy, easily tired; I adored luxury,
and should have been an extrovert; I usually

managed to make myself pretty comfortable. . . .
Well,' she laughed, 'we both were glad to dazzle.
A genius temperament should be handled with care.'

5 Onion Skin

It's the fancy functional things love us best;
not mutely useful, or austerely useless,
they touch our body to assume a body—
my half-pound silver ticker with two bopped lids,
a sliver lever to be thumbnailed out
at *six* or *six*, when all hands stop and time.
My watch ran to the clockmaker once too often.
Where's Grandfather's gold chain with the snake-head?
They go a-begging; without us they are lost.
This typing paper pulped in Bucksport, Maine,
onion skin, only merchandised in Maine,
creased when I pulled the last sheet, and seemed to scream,
as if Fortuna bled in the white wood,
first felt the bloody gash that brought me life.

Through The Night

1

The pale green leaves cling white to the lit night:
this has been written, and eaten out on carbons;
incendiaries strike no spark from this moonlight;
nothing less nutritive than the thirst at Harvard. . . .
Like the generation of leaves, the race of man;
their long hair, beads, jeans, are early uniforms,
rebellion that honors the liturgies.
I wake now, find myself this long alone,
left at nine by the curb at Quincy House,
waiting for my lift; it's the same for me
at fifty as at thirteen, my childish thirst
to be the grown-up in his open car and girl. . . .
She straddles the hood and snuffs the dust of twilight:
'I want to live,' she screams, 'where I can see.'

2

The thick-skinned leaf flickers along its veins
and shakes a little on the stiff, tense twig,
dancing its weekend jig in blood—Thank God;
for at the window of my house I looked,
I saw you walking with the simple ones,
in the twilight, in the evening, in the black, in the night;
not loud nor stubborn—and how earnestly,
I looked and found you lying on your bed;
you caught me and kissed me and stopped my rush,
your sinewy lips wide-eyed as the honeycomb,
your tongue as smooth as truth, your record-player

singing Gluck's *Orfeo*, the contralto's
'Where shall I go without Euridice?'
dying in our undergrowth, dense beyond reward.

3

The vague, dark new hallway, some darker rectangle:
the bathroom door, or a bedroom, someone else's;
tune of the wrong snoring, or, worse, the right—
each footstep a moral judgment, and the window
holds out its thin, black terminal disk of joy,
its blissfully withdrawing glimmer of immoral
retribution, as I lie awake basking,
trying to extend the dark, unspent minute,
as the window frame gradually burns green;
three panes still beam the polar blue of night,
as my backbone swims in the sperm of gladness,
as your figure emerges from your body,
we are two species, even from the inside—
a net trapped in the arms of another net.

4

Gradually greener in the window frame:
the old oil, unfamiliar here, alive
in a hundred eighteenth-century parks and landscapes—
Sir Joshua Reynolds might retouch each fault:
the cow-faced hound, the lonely, stalwart girl,
the scarlet general, more oaken than his oaks—
leaf, branch and trunk arranged as only money
and nobility, both somewhat outlaw here,
could render appropriate to the neighborhood:
one great window, one bright watching eye—
as achingly I awake to go the home-walk,

each pane, each windshield, familiar, unfamiliar,
each shingled, checkered window is sheer face,
the blindingly visible breasts freckle to brilliance.

5

Sloping, torn tarpaper on a wet roof,
on several roofs; here and there, a stray nail,
background of wrecked gingerbread Gothic,
a pop-art playground of psychedelic reds,
suburbia joining the Frontier. My judge was there:
cheeks of red brick powder, coarse horsetail hair,
Saint-Just, or anyone's nameless, mercantile
American ancestor of 1790—
head bowed, an elbow spiked on each sharp knee,
the cleansing guillotine peeping over his shoulder;
I climb the ladder, knowing my last words,
no matter how unjust, no longer matter,
the black marks of my nights erased in blood—
wondering, 'Why was it ever worth my while?'

6 *The Duc de Guise*

The grip gets puffy, and water wears the stones—
O to be always young among our friends,
as one of the countless peers who graced the world
with their murders and *joie de vivre*, made good
in a hundred aimless amorous bondages. . . .
As some great hero, Henri, Duc de Guise,
forge and Achilles of the Holy League,
whose canopy and cell we saw at Blois,
just before he died, at the moment of orgasm,
his round eyes, hysterical and wistful,
a drugged bull's breathing, a cool, well-pastured brain,

muscular slack of his stomach swelling
as if he were pregnant . . . before he sprang, his sword
unable to encircle the circle of his killers.

7

The green paint's always peeling from the prospect:
a man of eighty with the health of sixty,
strolling his lawn shaved smooth as a putting green—
this scene I could touch once, as I touch your hand,
our mirage future, keys jingling on the sky's
blue smoke-ring. How many enthusiasts are gone;
their bound legs march, the impudent standards
part the dust of the field, the fog of battle;
and the heart's moisture goes up like a summer drought.
We are firemen smashing holes in our own house.
We will each breath, and make our peace with war,
yearning to swoop with the swallow's brute joy,
indestructible as mercy—the round green weed
slipping free from the disappointment of the flower.

The Muse

1 Nantucket: 1935
(TO FRANK PARKER)

She never married, because she loved to talk,
'You watch the waves *woll* and *woll* and *woll* and *woll*,'
she lisped, and that was how we picked Nantucket.
I watched but little, though I tried the surf,
hung dead on its moment of infinity,
corked between water, sky and gravel, smothered,
smitten loose from volition. When I breathe now,
I hear that distant pant of gulls in my chest,
but death then was our classmate killed skidding on
a Vineyard sand-swerve—a first death, and its image:
your seascape of Moses breaking the Ten Commandments
against a mount of saltgrass, dune and surf,
repainted, then repainted, till the colors browned
to a whirl of mud in the hand of Michelangelo.

2 The Muses of George Grosz

Berlin in the twenties left the world behind
elsewhere the music crept, the paintings stank;
the iron hand of politics had clenched—
our artists too, they rush to break the windows,
as if we'd limped past Germany at last.
Groszmen are one man, Marshal von Hindenburg,
from crib to Methuselah, paying gold for Venus;
Groszmen never strip—Grosz women always:
girls one might meet at Modern Language Annuals,
pushing retirement, weighing more than men;

and once the least were good for the all-night game—
if one could swing the old sow by her tits:
the receding hairline of her nettled cunt
severed like the scalplock by the stroke of a brush.

Randall Jarrell: 1914-1965

1

Sixty, seventy, eighty: I see you mellow,
unchanging cricket, whistling down the grass-fires;
the same hair, snow-shocked, and wrist for tennis; now
   doubles,
not singles. . . . Who dares bridge that deadfall, sit
by you, watch the ivy turn, a wash of blood
on the infirmary wall, the sixth age autumn,
see the years wrinkling up the reservoir?
Students waiting for Europe and spring term to end,
we saw below us, golden, small, stockstill,
cornfields and polo field, the feudal campus airdrome,
its Georgian Trust; behind, above us, castle,
towers, dorms, fieldhouse, bishop's house and chapel—
Randall, the same fall lunges on the windshield,
the same apples ripen on the whiplash bough.

2

Grizzling on the embers of our onetime life,
our first intoxicating disenchantments,
dipping our hands once, twice, in the same river,
entrained for college on the Ohio local;
the scene shifts, middle distance, back and foreground,
things changing position like chessmen on a wheel,
drawn by a water buffalo, perhaps
blue with true space before the dawn of days—
then the night of the caged squirrel on its wheel:
lights, eyes, peering at you from the overpass;

black-gloved, black-coated, you plod out stubbornly,
as if asleep, Child Randall, as if in chainstep,
meeting the cars, and approving; a harsh luminosity,
as you clasp the blank coin at the foot of the tunnel.

Munich 1938

Hitler, Mussolini, Daladier, Chamberlain:
that historic confrontation of the great—
firm on one thing, they were against the war;
each won there, by shoving the war ahead twelve months.
Is it worse to choke on the vomit of cowardice,
or blow the world up on a point of honor? . . .
John Crowe Ransom at Kenyon College, Gambier, Ohio,
looking at primitive African art on loan:
gleam-bottomed naked warriors of oiled brown wood,
makeshift tin straws in their hands for spears;
far from the bearded, armored, all-profile hoplites
on the Greek vase; not distant maybe from their gods—
John saying, 'Well, they may not have been good neighbors,
but they never troubled the rest of the world.'

August 22, 1968

October and November

1 Che Guevara

Week of Che Guevara, hunted, hurt,
held prisoner one lost day, then gangstered down
for gold, for justice—violence cracking on violence,
rock on rock, the corpse of the last armed prophet
laid out on a sink in a shed, revealed by flashlight—
as the leaves light up, still green, this afternoon,
and burn to frittered reds; as the oak, branch-lopped
to go on living, swells with goiters like a fruit-tree,
as the sides of the high white stone buildings over-
shadow the poor, too new in the new world,
Manhattan, where our clasped, illicit hands
pulse, stop the bloodstream as if it hit rock. . . .
Rest for the outlaw . . . kings once hid in oaks,
with prices on their heads, and watched for game.

2 Caracas I

Through another of our cities without a center, as hideous
as Los Angeles, and with as many cars
per head, and past the 20-foot neon sign
for *Coppertone* on a church, past the population
earning $700 per capita
in jerry skyscraper living-slabs, and on to the White House
of El Presidente Leoni, his small men with 18-
inch repeating pistols, firing 45 bullets a minute,
the two armed guards petrified beside us, while we had
    champagne,
and someone bugging the President: 'Where are the girls?'

And the enclosed leader, quite a fellow, saying,
'I don't know where yours are, but I know where to find
   mine.' . . .
This house, this pioneer democracy, built
on foundations, not of rock, but blood as hard as rock.

3 The March I

(FOR DWIGHT MACDONALD)

Under the too white marmoreal Lincoln Memorial,
the too tall marmoreal Washington Obelisk,
gazing into the too long reflecting pool,
the reddish trees, the withering autumn sky,
the remorseless, amplified harangues for peace—
lovely to lock arms, to march absurdly locked
(unlocking to keep my wet glasses from slipping)
to see the cigarette match quaking in my fingers,
then to step off like green Union Army recruits
for the first Bull Run, sped by photographers,
the notables, the girls . . . fear, glory, chaos, rout . . .
our green army staggered out on the miles-long green fields,
met by the other army, the Martian, the ape, the hero,
his new-fangled rifle, his green new steel helmet.

4 The March II

Where two or three were heaped together, or fifty,
mostly white-haired, or bald, or women . . . sadly
unfit to follow their dream, I sat in the sunset
shade of their Bastille, the Pentagon,
nursing leg- and arch-cramps, my cowardly,
foolhardy heart; and heard, alas, more speeches,
though the words took heart now to show how weak
we were, and right. An MP sergeant kept

repeating, 'March slowly through them. Don't even brush
anyone sitting down.' They tiptoed through us
in single file, and then their second wave
trampled us flat and back. Health to those who held,
health to the green steel head . . . to your kind hands
that helped me stagger to my feet, and flee.

5 Charles Russell Lowell: 1835-1864

Hard to exhume him from the other Union martyrs;
though common now, his long-short, crisping hair,
his green mustache, the manly, foppish coat—
more and more often he turns up as a student:
twelves horses killed under him—a nabob cousin
bred, then shipped replacements. He had, *gave* . . . every-
    thing
at Cedar Creek—his men dismounted, firing
repeating carbines; heading two vicious charges,
the slug collapsing his bad, tubercular lung:
fainting, bleeding, loss of voice above a whisper;
Phil Sheridan—any captain since Joshua—shouting:
'I'll sleep in the enemy camp tonight, or hell. . . .'
Charles had himself strapped to the saddle . . . bound to death,
his cavalry that scorned the earth it trod on.

6 Caracas II

With words handled like the new grass writhing, rippling
in an urban brook, greens washed to double greenness—
one could get through life, though mute, with courage
and a merciful heart—two things, and a third thing:
humor . . . as the turned-out squatter clings
with amused bravery that takes the form of mercy
to the Old Square in Caracas, his shaky, one-man hovel,

the spoiled baroque cathedral from the age of Drake.
The church has hay in its courtyard; householders own the
    Common—
conservatives reduced to conservation:
green things, the well, the school, the writhing grass;
the communist committed to his commune,
artist and office-holder to a claque of less
than fifty souls . . . to each his venomous in-group.

Autumn in the Abstract

1 Alba

The building's color is fresh unfinished wood like
an old penny postcard; thirty stories seem hundreds,
with miniature view-windows that gleam like cells;
on a wafer balcony, too thin for human sitters,
hangs a crimson blazer, a replica
of the one I wear, but this is hollow, blows
to the fall air, shines with a Harvard shield. . . .
Eve and Adam, adventuring from the ache
of the first sleep, met forms less primitive
and honest, when they gazed on the stone-ax
and Hawaiian fig-leaf hanging from their fig-tree. . . .
Nothing more established, pure and lonely,
than the early Sunday morning in New York—
the sun on high burning, and most cars dead.

2 In Sickness

The desultory, commercial fall
lies like a mustard plaster on our backs,
determines us to labor, crave and pay. . . .
If I look for the unbelievably beautiful
in a city, it's mostly women in their war-paint—
the brave stands buckled to his scourge of armor,
the chemist smiles etherealized in his glass case.
Sometimes, my mind is a rocked and dangerous bell,
I climb the spiral steps to my own music;
a friend drops in the street and no one stirs.
Pavlov's dogs, when tortured, turned neurotics;

the cure: rest, exercise, fresh air and meals.
When we are brainwashed, we have read the book. . . .
In sickness, mind and body make a marriage.

3 Deutschland über Alles

Hitler, though we laugh, gave them the start,
the step forward, one had to give them that:
the Duce's, 'Once they start marching, they'll never stop.'
Joy in the introversion of loneliness,
the silver reichsmark sticking to the heel,
the knights corrupted by their purity,
made wilder by the wildness of the woodcut—
his eyes were glowing coals, the world turned dark,
the horde, on stopwatch, asked for earth and water,
settled for *lebensraum*, then *lebensraum*:
spaces, a space, the night astride the eyetooth.
Who will contest the conqueror his dirt,
spaces enough to bury what they left,
the six million Jews gassed in the space to breathe?

4 End of the Saga

'Even if they will murder the whole world,
we'll hit them so hard, they'll never tell the story.'
Kriemhild was shouting, 'If they get to the air,
and cool their coats of mail, we are all lost.'
Then the great hall was fired; we saw them kneel
beside their corpses, and drink the flowing blood—
unaccustomed to such drink, they thought it good,
in the great heat, it tasted cooler than wine.
They tried to lift their brothers from the fire,
they found them too hot to hold, and let them drop.
'O why are we so wet with our lifeblood?'

they asked. 'Our bones are broken, not our hearts. . . .'
The king is laughing, all his men are killed,
he is shaken by the news, as well he might be.

Symbols

1 The Well

The stones of the well were sullenly unhewn,
none could deny their leechlike will to stay—
no dwelling near and four square miles of flatness,
pale grass diversified by wounds of sand,
the grass as hard as rock and squeezed by winter,
each well-stone rounded as an ostrich egg,
strange for unfinished stone. It seemed a kind
of dead chimney. Any halting boy
was free to pitch the bucket, drinking cup
and funnel down the well—his neighbor's bucket
through bottomless, thin black hoops of standing water,
and plenty of elbowroom for scuttled gear;
room to reach the bottom, unnoticed, undented. . . .
It's not the crowds, but crowding kills the soul.

2 Hell

'Circles of Dante—and in that dirt-roofed cave,
each family had marked off its yard of space;
no light except their coal fires laid in buckets,
no draft of air except their smoke, no water,
no hole to hide the excrement. I walked on,
afraid of stumbling on the helpless bodies,
afraid of circling. I soon forgot the Fascist
or German deserters I was hunting—screaming
children, old men, old women, coughing and groaning.
Then hit my head on the low dirt, and reached out
to keep from falling or hurting anyone;

and what I touched was not the filthy floor:
a woman's hand returning my quick grasp,
her finger tracing the lifeline on my palm.'

3 Rats

A friend of that day, the Black Muslim
on our masons' gang at the Danbury Jail,
held his hand over the postcard Connecticut
landscape, scarred by us and a few mean human
houses, *Only man is miserable.*
He was wrong though, he forgot the rats. A pair
in an enclosure kills the rest, then breeds a clan.
Stranger rats with their wrong clan-smell stumble
on the clan, are run squeaking with tails and backs split open
up trees and fences—to die of nervous shock.
Someone rigged the enclosure with electric levers
that could give the rats an orgasm. Soon the rats learned
to press the levers, did nothing else—still on the trip,
they died of starvation in a litter of food.

4 In the Cage

The lifers file into the hall,
according to their houses—twos
of laundered denim. On the wall
a colored fairy tinkles blues
and titters by the balustrade;
canaries chip the bars, and scream.
We come from tunnels where the spade
pickax and hod for plaster steam
in mud and insulation. Here
the Bible-twisting Israelite
fasts for his Harlem. It is night.

and it is vanity; the age
numbs the failed nerve for service. Fear,
the yellow chirper, beaks its cage.

Winter 1944 [from *Lord Weary's Castle*]

5 *The River God*

The Aztecs gave the human sacrifice
credit-cards, dames, the usual pork of kings;
after a year, the king was cooled with palm-slash;
none ever detected he had lost his heart—
the gods and the sun were succored by his blood. . . .
Mao had to find ways to economize on lepers;
each family had a leper, fed it like a pig;
Mao announced the people's plan for leprosy,
the lepers came bounding from the filth of hiding,
more lepers than Jordan or Tigris ever washed,
from Naaman to the popular cures of Christ . . .
Then doped like kings, the boatride colorful,
launched on the Yangtze with a thousand flowers—
the river god caught them in his arms when they drowned.

6 *The Leak*

We must have seven-league boots to cross these tiles;
drops strike with the tock of the town clock,
then more rapidly than the second hand;
it's like industry's dogged, clogged pollution—
a soaked roll of tissue, scored like a Moslem tile,
your saturated, crested bathmat, wadded
to a sprinkling pipe and alchemized to water;
in the basin, a gold ringlet of pubic hair. . . .
I hear their water torture, running rivers:
Let us cross over the river and rest under the trees. . . .

We open the window, and there is no view,
no green meadow pointing to *the* green meadow,
to dogs, to deer, Diana in her war-skirt. . . .
Heaven must be paved with terra-cotta tile.

For Aunt Sarah

You never had the constitution to quarrel:
poised, warm and cool, distrusting beards and greatness,
yet infinitely kind—in short a lady,
still reaching past the turn of the century
for your youth in that solid golden age, when means
needed only to follow the golden mean
to guide and have the world; when the businessmen
and their crews of statesmen willingly gave up
health, wealth and pleasure for the cell of office,
guided by their only fiction, God.
But this new age? 'They have no fun,' you say. . . .
We've quarreled lightly almost fifty years,
Dear, long enough to know how high our pulse beats, while
    the young
wish to stand in our shoes before we've left them.

The Heavenly Rain

Man is the root of everything he builds;
no nature, except the human, loves New York—
the clerk won't prove Aseity's existence
running from helpless cause to helpless cause. . . .
The rain falls down from heaven, and heaven keeps
her noble distance, the dancer, seen not heard.
The rain falls down, the soil swims up to breathe,
the squatter sumac, shafted in cement,
flirts its wet leaves to heaven like the Firebird.
Two girls clasp hands in a clamshell courtyard to watch
the weed of the sumac aging visibly;
the girls age not, are always young as last week,
wish all rains one rain—this, that will not wash
the fallen leaf, turned scarlet, back to green.

Charles River

1

The sycamores throw shadows on the Charles,
while the fagged insect splinters to rejoin
the infinite, now casting its loose leaf
on the short-skirted girl and long-haired escort,
and the black stream curves, as if it led a lover—
not so our blood: in workaday times,
one takes cold comfort in its variations,
its endless handspring round the single I,
the thumping and pumping of overfevered zeal;
but for a week our blood has pointed elsewhere:
it brings us here tonight, and ties our hands—
if we leaned forward, and should dip a finger
into this river's momentary black flow,
the infinite small stars would break like fish.

2

The circuit of those snow-topped rural roads, eight miles
to ten, might easily have been the world's
top, round the pole, when I trailed on spreading skis
my guide, his unerring legs ten inches thick in wool,
and pinched my earlobes lest they turn to snowdrops—
hard knocks to school a lifetime; yet I went on swiping
small things. That knife, snow-yellow with eleven blades,
where is it now? It will outlast us all,
though flawed already when I picked it up. . . .
And now, the big town river, once hard and dead as its
  highways,

rolls blackly into country river, root-banks, live ice,
a live muskrat muddying the moonlight. You trail me,
Woman, so small, if one could trust the appearance,
I might be in trouble with the law.

3

My father's letter to your father, saying
tersely and much too stiffly that he knew
you'd been coming to my college rooms alone—
I can still almost crackle that slight note in my hand.
I see your outraged father; you, his outraged daughter;
myself brooding in fire and a dark quiet
on the abandoned steps of the Harvard Fieldhouse,
calming my hot nerves and enflaming my mind's
nomad quicksilver by saying *Lycidas*—
then punctiliously handing the letter to my father.
I knocked him down. He half-reclined on the carpet;
Mother called from the top of the carpeted stairs—
our glass door locking behind me, no cover; you
idling in your station wagon, no retreat.

4

There was rebellion, Father, when the door slammed . . .
front doors were glass then . . . and you hove backward
    rammed
into the heirlooms, screens, the sun-disk clock,
the highboy quaking to its toes . . . father,
I do not know how to unsay I knocked you down.
I've breathed the seclusion of your glass-tight den,
card laid by a card until the pack was used,
old Helios turning the arid plants to blondes,
woman's life sentence on each step misplaced.

I have blown moondust in the mouth of the rich;
you then, further from death than I am, knew
the student ageless in a green cloud of hash,
her pad, three boxbeds half a foot off floor—
far as her young breasts half a foot away.

5

If the clock had stopped in 1936
for them, or again in '50 and '54—
they are not dead, and not until death parts us,
will I stop sucking my blood from their hurt.
They say, 'I had my life when I was young.'
They must have . . . dying young in middle-age;
yet often the old grow still more beautiful,
watering out the hours, biting back their tears,
as the white of the moon streams in on them unshaded;
and women too, the tanning rose, their ebb,
neither a medical, nor agricultural problem.
I struck my father; later my apology
hardly scratched the surface of his invisible
coronary . . . never to be effaced.

6

Longer ago than we had lived till then,
before the *Anschluss*, the thirty or forty million
war-dead . . . but who knows now off hand how many?
I tasted first love gazing through your narrow
bay window at the hideous concrete dome
of M.I.T., the last blanched, hectic glow
sunset-blackened on the bay of the Esplanade:
an imperial shrine in a landscape by Claude Lorrain,
an artist out of fashion, like Nero, his Empire

of heaven-vaulting aqueducts, baths, arches,
roads, legions, plowshares beaten down to swords,
the blood of the spirit lost in veins of brickdust—
Christ also, our only king without a sword,
turning the word forgiveness to a sword.

7

No stars worth noticing; the lights of man
lunge road and sky; and life is wild here: straw
puts teeth in the shore strip; the water smells and lives.
We walk our tightrope, this embankment, jewed—
no, yankeed—by the highways down to a grassy lip. . . .
Once—you weren't born then—an iron railing,
charmless and dignified, policed this walk;
it matched the times, and had an esplanade,
stamping down grass and growth with square stone shoes;
the Charles itself, half ink, half liquid coaldust,
testified to the health of industry—
wrong times, an evil dispensation; yet who
can hope to enter heaven with clean hands?
A groan went up when the iron railing crashed.

8

No outward and visible sign, the sleep unbroken,
except when winds thrust through the smooth stone cube,
our bedroom, putty-gray and putty-cool. . . .
A car or two, then none; or always none.
Roads on three levels parallel the river,
roads pace the river in a losing struggle,
forces of nature trying to breathe beneath
the jacket of lava. We lie parallel,
parallel to the river, parallel

to six roads—unmoving and awake,
awake and naked, like a line of Greeks
facing a second line of Greeks—like them,
willing to enter the battle, and not come out . . .
morning's useful traffic . . . the unbroken snore.

Thanksgiving

1 Ulysses and Nausicaa

In the same long hair, gay, dirty clothes—one sex,
arm on shoulders, searing the autumn summer,
Shakespeare extras by cars, the oars of the Charles—
there's a new poetry in the air, it's youth's
patent, lust coolly led on by innocence.
Gardens, how far from Eden fallen, though
still fair! *Hoc opus, hic labor est*—the lust
of Ulysses landhugging from port to port for girls. . . .
Is marriage a cover for the underworld,
dark harbor of suctions and the second chance,
not Nausicaa found twenty years too late?
Scarred husband and wife sit naked, one Greek smile,
because their ships are burned and all friends lost.
How we wish we were friends with half our friends!

2 Marching

When life grows shorter and daylightsaving dies,
God's couples marched in arms to harvest home,
to Plymouth's communal distilleries—
three days they lay at peace with God and beast. . . .
They reel, arms locked, from luncheon into night:
bellbottom, barefoot, Christendom's wild hair;
words are what get in the way of what they say.
Youth's mobile, but no friend of the waste leaf.
None sleeps with the same girl twice, or marches homeward,
keeping the beat of her arterial vein,
or hears the cello grumbling in her garden.

The sleeper has learned karate—Revolution,
drugging her terrible premenstrual cramps,
marches with unbra'd breasts to storm the city.

3 Romanoffs

'Let's face it, English is a racist redoubt.'
We plead guilty, the laws of history tell us
irrelevant things that happen never happened.
Blacks and Reds survive, but where is White?
The word has vanished from the English tongue,
a class wiped out, its legacy, one-existence,
no calendar updated in their favor.
Arrogance gives the mighty solitude
to study the desolation of their thought—
starred cellar, where they shot and then dismembered
Tsar, Tsarina, the costly hemophyllic children—
'Those statesmen,' said Lenin, 'sent 16 million to death.'
These fairy stories served my brainwashed youth—
we, the Romanoffs with much to lose.

4 Two Farmers

A nose flat-bent, not hawk, cheeks razored sand—
Velásquez' self-portrait is James MacDonald,
Jim to grandfather, MacDonald to the children,
though always *Mr.* in our vocative.
Having one's farmer then was like owning a car.
He sits on his lawn waiting a lift to the Old Men's Home;
saying? Here even the painter's speaking likeness ends;
nor could he paint my grandfather. I've overtaken
most of the elders of my youth, not this one,
yet I begin to know why he stood the frost
so many weekends with his little grandson

sawing up his trees for a penny a log—
Old Cato, ten years to live, preferring this squander
to his halcyon Roman credit from the Boom.

Le Vieux Caton

My telephone swings crippled to solitude
two feet from my ear; as so often and so often,
I hold your dialogue away to breathe—
still this is love, not Old Cato foregoing his wife,
only jumping her in thunderstorms like *Juppiter Tonans*;
frankness gave him long, bright days of silence,
then deafness changed his gifts for rule to genius.
Saint-Just thought *empire goes to the phlegmatic*;
Cato knew from the Greeks that empire is hurry,
when he held a bunch of ripe African figs in the Senate:
Cartago delenda! That New York of her day. . . . He knew
a blindman hunting a ring in a pile of dust
must grab the dust; trade needs no kick from a rival;
Rome, if built at all, must be built in a day.

Names

1 Sir Thomas More

Hans Holbein's More, my friend since World War II,
the gold chain of S's, the golden rose,
the plush cap, the brow's damp feathertips of hair,
the slate eyes' stern, facetious twinkle, ready
to turn from executioner to martyr—
or saunter with the great King's bluff arm on his neck,
feeling that friend-slaying, terror-ridden heart
beating under the fat of Aretino—
some hanger-on saying, 'How the King must love you!'
And Thomas, 'If it were a question of my head,
or losing his meanest village in France. . . .' Or standing
below the scaffold and the two-edged sword—
'Friend, help me up,' he said, 'when I come down,
my head and body will shift for themselves.'

2 Marcus Cato the Younger

Cato too, a boy still, at Sulla's villa, the tombs,
saw people come in as men, and leave as heads.
'Why hasn't someone killed him?' he asked. They answered,
'Men fear Sulla even more than they hate him.'
'Give me a sword.' Thereafter his word was a sword;
drowning Plato and wine all night with friends,
gambling his life in the Forum, stoned like Paul,
he went on speaking while the soldiers saved their State,
saved Caesar. . . . At the last cast of his lost cause,
he bloodied his hand on a slave who hid his sword;
he fell in a small sleep, then heard the small birds chirping.

His sprained hand struck. When they put back his bowels,
he tore them with his own hands. . . . He's where he would be:
a Roman who died, perhaps, for Rome.

3 Joinville and Louis IX

'Given my pilgrim's scarf and staff, I left
the village of Joinville on foot, barefoot, in my shirt,
never turning my eyes for fear my heart would melt
at leaving my mortgaged castle, my two fair children—
a Crusader? Some of us lived, and many ransomed
bishops, nobles and Brothers of the King
strolled free in Acre, and begged the King to sail home,
and desert the meaner folk. Sore of heart then,
I went to a barred window, and passed my arms through the
     bars
of the window, and someone came, and leant on my shoulders,
and placed his two hands on my head. "Philip of Nemours,"
I screamed, "leave me in peace!" The hands fell by chance,
and I knew the King by the emerald on his hand:
"If I should leave Jerusalem, who will remain?" '

4 Alexander

His sweet moist eye missed nothing—the vague guerrilla,
untested ground, the tested tactic, the hell-fire drive,
the pundit knotting his net of dialectic—
his phalanxes kept oiled ten years for the crux of battle,
his engines engineered to the fall of Tyre—
Achilles . . . but in Aristotle's corrected copy—
health burning like the dewdrop on that flesh
hit in a hundred calculated sallies,
to give the Persians the cup of love, his brothers—
the wine-bowl of the Macedonian drinking bout . . .

drinking out of friendship, then meeting Medius,
then drinking, then bathing, then sleeping, then meeting
    Medius,
then drinking, then bathing . . . dead at thirty-two—
in this life only is our hope in Christ.

5 Napoleon

Boston's used bookshops, anomalies from London, are gone;
hard even now to fathom why I spent
my vacations lugging home the third-hand *Lives*—
shaking the dust from that stationary stock:
myopic lithograph, and gilt-edged pulp
on a man—not bloodthirsty, not sparing of blood;
with the ways and means to manage everything;
his iron hand, no soft appendage to his brain,
fell with the mortal quickness of his lust,
uprooting races, kingdoms, Jacobins—
the price was paltry . . . three million soldiers dead,
grand opera fixed like morphine in their veins.
Dare I say, he had no moral center?
All gone like the smoke of his own artillery?

6 Waterloo

Hung thunderclouded over the mantel of our summer
cottage by the owners, Miss Barnard or Mrs. Curtis:
a sad engraving, half life-scale, removed now, and no doubt
wrecked as too imperial and raw for our stomachs:
Waterloo, Waterloo! You could choose sides then:
the French uniforms, a blue-black, came out black,
the British Redcoats gray; those running were French—
one, an aide-de-camp, Napoleon's clearly, wore
a waterfall of overstated braid,

there sabered, dying, his standard wrenched from weak hands
by his killer, a helmeted, fog-gray dragoon,
the true Britannia, the rib of oak—
six centuries, this field of their encounter,
La Gloire changing to *sauve qui peut* and *merde*.

Harvard

1

Beauty-sleep for the writer, and the beauty,
both fighting off muscular cramps, the same fatigue.
Lying in bed, letting the bright, white morning
rise to mid-heaven through a gag of snow,
through highschool, through college, through fall-term vaca-
    tion—
I've slept so late here, snow has stubbled my throat;
students in their hundreds rise from the beehive,
swarm-mates; they have clocks and instincts, make
classes. In the high sky, a parochial school,
the top floors looking like the Place des Vosges—
a silk stocking, blown thin as smog, coils in a twig-fork,
dangling a wire coathanger, rapier-bright—
a long throw for a hard cold day . . . wind lifting
the stocking like the lecherous, lost leg.

2

Each hour the stocking thins, the hanger dulls;
cold makes the school's green copper cupola
greener over the defoliated playground;
clouds lie in cotton wads on the Dutch sky,
an end to the epic lays of dwarf and giant,
the dirt of students and the doctor's pearls.
My mind can't hold the focus for a minute,
I bear the dark of the moon on the white of my eye,
flash-visions the hooded projector will not hold—
my *Absence* is present . . . her black fishnet leg,

curve of the hourglass standing by the shower,
the stoned garrulity of her white lips—
Isaiah's! Who will sit the sermon out?
The new blade is too sharp, the old poisons.

3

The gluttony of eating out alone
here in Cambridge, where anyone can be no one,
and the people we'd flee at dinner parties change
to the mysterious, the beautiful . . . .
I on display on my small table, overwhite,
overobserved, ignored . . . the moment tries
my soul grown seasick on cold loneliness—
swimmer sinking short of Labrador;
yet everyone who is seated is a lay,
or Paul Claudel. He's near me now, declaiming:
'*L'Académie Groton, eh, c'est une école admirable,*'
soaring from hobbled English to a basic French,
a vocabulary poorer than Racine's . . .
minataur steaming in a maze of eloquence.

4

Inching along the bayfront on the icepools,
sea and shipping cut out by the banks of cars,
and our relationship advancing or
declining to private jokes, and chaff and lust. . . .
Our leeway came so seldom, fell so short,
overwatched by some artist's skylight in the city,
or some suburban frame-house basement window,
angular, night-bluish, blear-eyed, spinsterish—
still this is something, something we can both
take hold of willingly, go smash on, if we will:

all flesh is grass, and like the flower in the field;
no! lips, breasts, eyes, hands, lips, hair;
as the overworked central heating bangs the frame,
as a milkhorse in childhood, would crash the morning milk-
    can.

Alcohol

1

Suddenly, no disinclination to murder—
brown hours, they stream like water off my back.
I want to top the crowns of the tallest flowers
with the blade of a hand, sweep, sweep and down-sweep,
running in bull-horns down the garden path,
pretending left, right and wrong are in the wind. . . .
Harder to be an audience than on stage,
live in the small unknown Horatian suburb:
the lawn is skinned, the wife tensed, the great torrent
lost in the melancholy stream of traffic.
I live in the sun, and my lips keep twitching.
I suffer more for myself than I do for you
burning in the sun of the universal bottle;
and the spineless vermin slink and stink in the woodwork.

2

Pale ale, molar drain . . . I face the men's room mirror,
walrus mustaches, or antlers, two bad tusks.
I am clean-shaven, love the all-clear of shaving—
make the girls love, not war, and make the girls. . . .
I am a worshipper of myth and monster:
faces hairy as coal-drift shredded wheat,
old soaks murdered by the depilated stripling,
his genitalia hairless bowling balls.
Comb never bruised the hair of John the Baptist;
or was it Samson? Was it alcohol
never passed his lips? Moses saw the Mountain

lift his bullet-head past timberline to heaven.
In the Gardens of Allah, man still wears the beard,
the women are undressed, accepting love.

3

Nature might do her thing for us; so they swore,
with peeled staff, imbecility and psalter
scrounging Northumberland for the infinite—
camping on a shorefront where the dusk seal
nightly dog-paddles on the hawk for fish,
whiskering giddy the harbor, a black blanket
patched up with splotches of the sky, the sky,
bluebird and blackbird blending into black;
where the Brook Trout dolphins by the housepiles,
grows common by mid-vacation as hamburger,
its fish-translucence cooked to white of an egg—
to see the young yachts, half your income, come
about at your bulwark—they, no longer than your car;
you are no larger than the shoe you fit.

In the Forties

1

The back-look? Green logs sizzled on the fire-dogs,
painted scarlet like British Redcoats. June
steamed up in greenness; in the sopping trees
the green frog whistled to the greener sigh
of the new leaf—jay and catbird afoot,
head cocked for earthworms in the sidewalk puddles—
and you, dear, coming to our house, where words
were seldom passed except in public. . . . Hot
from toiling up the Portland Wagon Road,
we saw the burial ground of the Abenaki,
French converts called the Praying Niggers, though
this helped them little with the English, who
scalped, killed and burned brave, squaw and child; then held
this field . . . as later we, newcomers, free.

2

The heron warped its neck, a broken pick,
to study its reflection in the glare
of the lily pads bright as mica, swarming
with plant-lice in the wood-blood water.
I held you, while your ballet glasses held
the heron twisted by a fist of alder,
your figure's synonym—a chest so thin then,
your ribs stood out like bars. . . . Great men had dwelt here,
lords of their self-inflicted desiccation,
roaming for passage through the virgin forest,
stalking a far more greenly brutal quarry

down the warpaths to wives and twenty children—
many of them, too many, love, to count . . .
born to fill up the graveyards . . . thick as sticks.

3

Even in August, it turned autumn . . . all
Prospect Pond could harbor. No sound; no talk;
the dead match nicked the water and expired,
a target-circle on inverted sky,
nature's mirror . . . just a little cold!
Our day was cold and short, love, and its sun,
numb as the red carp, twenty inches long,
panting, a weak old dog, below a smashed
oar floating from a metal dock. The fish
is fungus; we too wear a larger face.
I rowed for the reflection, but it slid
between my fingers aground. . . . There the squirrels,
conservatives and vegetarians,
hold their roots and freehold, love, unsliding.

Now

1. Candlelight Lunchdate

An oldtime sweatshop remodelled, purple brick—
our candlelightbulbs twinkle in stormlamp chimneys:
the *Chez Dreyfus,* Harvard. The chimneys are shaded, but
this life is savage. We're not highschool dates.
I hated the middle-aged, now middle age
is a year my senior, or ten years younger, twenty—
Mr. Catman, Mr. Bigman on the Campus.
Say the worst of it, Cambridge speaks English,
words are given a fighting chance to speak:
her hand now unattainable was not attained.
'You used to be less noisy.' Hell means bright lights,
I can still find beautiful dyed gold hair in the field.
We needn't be sick in mind, or believe in God,
to love the flesh of our youth, V-mouth of the pike.

2. The Literary Life, a Scrapbook

My photo: I before I was I, or a book;
inch-worm! A cheekbone gumballs out my cheek;
too much live hair. My wife caught in that eye blazes,
an egg would boil in the tension of that hand,
my untied shoestrings write my name in the dust. . . .
I rest on a tree, and try to sharpen bromides
to serve the great, the great God, the New Critic,
who loves the writing better than we ourselves. . . .
In those days, if I pressed an ear to the earth,
I heard the bass growl of Hiroshima. No!
In the *Scrapbook,* it's the old who die classics:

one foot in the grave, two in books—one of the living!
Who wouldn't rather be his indexed correspondents
than the boy Keats spitting out blood for time to breathe?

Sleep

1

Four windows, five feet tall, soar up like windows,
rinsing their stained-glass angels in the void,
interminably alert for the four-hour stay till morning:
a watery dearth, made plain, and made to last
by a light or two hung on a telephone pole;
ashcan and alley, the makeshift rooming-house,
clawed from packing crates, and painted gray,
frozen interminably to this four-hour verge. . . .
Heaven? Time stops here too—Flesh of my Flesh,
elastic past the mind's agility,
hair coiled back on guard like the spring of a watch,
legs showing pale as wooden matches, lit
by four streak windows of the uncreating dawn,
not night or day, here stealing a brief life from both.

2

Six straight hours to teach on less than three hours' sleep—
I know I'll be smitten by the hand of my cells,
my gray hairs will not go down to the grave in peace. . . .
I get to know myself, a bluff and talker,
who cannot stand up to the final round. . . .
To enjoy the avarice of loneliness,
sleep the hour hand round the clock, stay home,
lie like a hound, on bounds for chasing a hound,
roped short in a spare corner, nose on paws,
one eyelid raised to guard the bowl of water;
panting, 'Better to die, than hate or fear,

better die twice than make ourselves feared or hated—
no, happier to live in a land without history,
where the bad-liver lives longer than his laws.'

3

An aquamarine bottle twinkles on a pane;
outside, a one-story factory with a spook chimney,
built in the age of trains and Robert Fulton,
condemned by law and Harvard, still alive.
A first tiger cat stationed on the record-player
spies on a second reaching from its carton-
dollhouse to bat a brass ball on a string;
the tree, untinseled, asymmetrical,
shoves up askewly blessing a small sprawl
of sealed, blank-papered Christmas packages;
your girl, she's nine still, comes wisely, inopportunely
reappearing—you standing up on your bed
in your Emily Dickinson nightgown, purely marveling
whether to be sensible or drown.

To Margaret Fuller Drowned

Earth of our pot I smashed dogs me four flights—
you are your biographer's best American woman,
in a white nightgown, hair fallen long
at the foot of the foremast, Margaret Fuller
forty, Angelo thirty, Angelino one—
drowned with brief anguish, together, and your fire-call.
Your voice was like thorns crackling under a pot,
you knew the Church loads and infects as all dead forms,
however brave and lovely in their life;
progress is not by renunciation.
'Ourselves,' you wrote, 'are all we know of heaven.
With the intellect, I always can
and always shall make out, but that's not half—
the life, the life, O my God, will life never be sweet?'

Henry and Waldo

Emerson is New England's Montaigne or Goethe,
very cold ginger, poison to Don Giovanni—
as on his winter lecture-jaunt with Thoreau,
red flannels, one bowl of broken ice for shaving;
few lives contained so many renunciations.
Thoreau, like Mallarmé and many another,
found life too brief for perfection and long for comfort;
his friend would sooner take the arm of an elmtree,
but he easily heard voices on the river,
wood groans from the banksand gliding of bark canoes,
twilight flaking through the manes of trees;
the color that killed him was perhaps a mouse,
zinc eating at the moonstalk, or the starlings
flocking and lighting, a dash of poisonous metal.

Dawn

The great dawn of Boston lifts from its black rag;
Thanksgiving to Christmas and a three-week rain,
winter Europe of moderate, night-black days—
blanch flesh! Too often my veins are mineral,
dirt-full as the arteries of a white cup;
I'm through with looking steadily at the worst—
Chaucer's old January made hay with May.
In this ever more enlightened room,
I wake beside the early rising sun,
sex indelible on the flowering air—
shouldn't I pray for us to hold forever,
body of dolphin, breast of cloud?
You rival the renewal of all seasons,
clearing the puddles with your last-year books.

Blizzard in Cambridge

Risen from the blindness of teaching to bright snow,
and everything mechanical stopped dead:
taxis thumbs-down on fares, tires burning the ice;
wet eye, iced-eyelash, spring-wear; subways held,
too jammed and late to wait for passengers;
to snow-trekking the mile from subway end to airport,
to all-flights-canceled, to the queues congealed
to telephones out of order, to the groping buses,
to rich, stranded New Yorkers staring with the wild, mild eyes
of steers at the foreign subway—then the train home,
rolling with stately grumbling: an hour in Providence,
another in New Haven—in darkness seeing
white arsenic numbers on the tail of a downed plane,
the smokestacks of abandoned fieldguns burning skyward.

Flight in the Rain

—Why does he say, I'm not afraid of flying?
—His imagination has lost the word for dying.
—It must be worse, if you have imagination. . . .
That night: the wing-tilt, air-bounce upright, lighted
Long Island mainstreets flashed like dice on the window;
the raindrop, gut troutlines wriggling on the window;
the landings, not landing; the long low flight at snailspace
exhausting a world of suburban similars. . . .
The sick stomach says, *You were*. Says, *Pray*—
this mismanaged life incorrigible. . . .
Prayer lives longer than God—God, the déja vû,
He sees the sparrow fall, heard years from here
in Rio, one propeller clunking off,
our *Deo gracias* on the puking runway.

Christmas and New Year

1 Snake

One of God's creatures, just as much as you,
or God; what other bends its back in crooks
and curves so gracefully, or yields a point;
brews a more scalding venom from cooler blood;
or flings its spine-string noosed about their throats:
hysterical bird, wild pig, or screaming rabbit?
Often I see it sunning on bright, brisk days,
when the heat has ebbed from its beloved rocks;
it is seamless, scaled-down to its integrity,
coiled for indiscriminate malevolence.
Lately, its hubris pushed it past man's patience;
stoned, flesh-chipped, it holds its hole now, sentenced
to hibernate fifty years. . . . It will thaw, then kill—
my little lamb in wolfskin, whip of wisdom.

2 Christmas Tree

Twenty or more big cloth roses, rose-color or scarlet,
coil in the branches—a winning combination
for you, who have gathered them eight years or more:
bosom-blossoms from Caribbean steambath forests,
changeless, though changed from tree to tree, unchanged
and transplants—like you, I think: twenty small birds or more,
nipping the needles; a quail, a golden warbler. . . .
And the others? Run of the mill; except for those minnowy
green things, no known species, made of woven straw:
little laundry hampers and steamer trunks for the elves.
A fine thing, built with love; though too unconventional

for our child to buy. . . . Who can bear the modesty
and righteousness of the woman's ego stripped naked:
'Because I lacked ambition, men thought me mad'?

3 The Dialogue

Old campaigner, I must surrender something,
tenting tonight and tenting under arms,
not talking for victory but survival—
only when we were assaulted were we Mongols;
meaning—let's forget the breakage—words.
You had just provocation: in the cool hour,
the monk and libertine kept swapping masks,
rough spice of cavalier and puritan.
How could we nurse one family glass of Bourbon
through two half hours of television news,
through striking teachers and the striking soldier
Red heaven pumped in heartbeats to my forehead,
the cherry rolling in the glass of sugared spirits . . .
How could two spirits get to bed on that?

4 Playing Ball with the Critic

(FOR RICHARD BLACKMUR)
We're trained to practice to kick the ball
to the police, and smile and even like it;
they too like it, smile and kick the ball;
the hurt blue muscles work like testicles;
where else can we learn to duck and block the knock?
'Is it a form of a force, or sentiment of a form?
His logic lacerates his vision, vision turns
his logic to zealotry,' or, 'In his first, best, book,
no poem offers a logical evaluation'—
still, it's a privilege to earn the bullring.

Quarrels seldom come from the first cause;
some small passage in our cups at dinner
rouses the Samuel Johnson in a wife,
sends us home kicking each bleeding leaf of the weeds.

5 George H. and George E. Lewes

A lady in bonnet, brow clearer than the Virgin,
the profile of a white rhinoceros—
but as for living, they left it to the servants,
and neither ever wished a second youth,
and neither wished to garden, since they thought
a garden is a grave, and drains the inkwell.
Theirs, Victorian England's one true marriage,
one Victorian England pronounced *Mormonage*;
a match between two virgins. Writers marry
their kind still, true and one and clashing, though lacking
the woman's dull gray eyes, vast pendulous nose,
her huge mouth, and jawbone which forbore to finish:
George Eliot's gracious, indifferent Tolstoyan gaze,
George Eliot without Tolstoy, the Countess Tolstoy.

6 The Book of Wisdom

Can I go on loving anyone at fifty,
still cool to the dense and five-times wounded lives
of those we loathed with wild idealism young?
Though the gods only toss me twenty cards,
twenty, thirty, or fifty years of work,
I shiver up vertical like a baby pigeon,
palate-sprung for the worm, senility—
to strap the gross artillery to my back,
lash on destroying what I lurch against,
not with anger, but unwieldy feet,

ballooning like the spotted, warty, blow-rib toad,
King Solomon croaking, 'This too is vanity;
her lips are a scarlet thread, her breasts are towers,'
hymns of the terrible organ in decay.

7 Trout

I lean by a bridgehead watching the clear calm,
a homeless sound of joy is in the sky:
a fisherman making falsecasts over a brook,
a two pound browntrout darting with scornful quickness,
drawing straight lines like arrows through the pool.
The man might as well break his rod in his fist,
his trembling boot or finger scares the fish;
trout will never hit flies in this brightness.
The man with the rod keeps watching on his bank,
he wades, he stamps his feet, he muddies the water;
before I know it, his rod begins to dip.
He wades, he stamps, he shouts to turn the run
of the trout with his wetfly breathed into its belly—
broken whiplash in the gulp of joy.

8 Descendant

The cloud of witnesses . . . they are flown like sundew,
and have left their debts to the widow and orphan;
to the virus crawling on its belly like a blot,
a hairbreadth an aeon, lives of love-in-death,
Venusberg in Venus fly-trap; to the tyrannosaur,
first carnivore to stand on its own feet,
to the Piltdown Man, first carnivore to laugh;
to the raised hand of Hitler, clenched fist of Stalin—
heaven descending from the hand of man.
But was there some shining, grasping hand to guide

me when I breathed through gills, and walked on fins
through Eden, plucking the law of retribution from the tree?
Did the Lord wish to enjoy the desolation?
Was the snake in the garden, an agent provocateur?

9 Bird

Aroused, then sleeping, caught adrift . . . the voice
singing to me in French, 'O mon avril.'
Those nasals . . . they woo us. Spring. Not theirs. Not mine.
A large pileated bird flies up,
dropping excretions like a frightened snake,
its Easter feathers; its earwax-yellow spoonbill
angrily hitting from side to side to blaze
a broad passage through the Great Northern Jungle—
the lizard tyrants were killed to a man by this bird,
man's forerunner. I pick up stones, and hope
to snatch its crest, its crown, at last, and cross
the perilous passage, sound in mind and body . . .
often reaching the passage, seeing my thoughts
stream on the water, as if I were cleaning fish.

10 Serpent

In my dream my belly was yellow, panels
of mellowing ivory, splendid and still young,
mellowing toward life-end like myself;
my green and brown backscales are cool to touch.
For one who has always loved snakes, it's no loss
to change to nature. My fall was elsewhere—
how often I made the woman bathe in her waters.
With daylight I turn small, a small snake
on the towpath writhing up the jags—
this path as often as the great clock clangs round,

I see me . . . the green hunter leaps from turn to turn,
a new brass bugle slung on the invisible baldric;
he is groping for trout in the private river,
wherever it opens, wherever it happens to open.

Mexico

1

The difficulties, the impossibilities,
stand out: I, fifty, humbled with the years' gold garbage,
dead laurel grizzling my back like spines of hay;
you, some sweet, uncertain age, say twenty-seven,
unballasted by honor or deception.
What help then? Not the sun, the scarlet blossom,
and the high fever of this seventh day,
the wayfarer's predestined diarrhea, nausea,
the multiple mosquito spots, round as pesos.
Hope not in God here, nor the Aztec gods;
we sun-people know the sun, the source of life,
will die, unless we feed it human blood—
we two are clocks, and only count in time;
the hand's knife-edge is pressed against the future.

2

Faith that neither quickstep, nor slowstep, nor charges fanned
by the flame of Allah, nor hope of saving wife and child
weigh much against their concentrated fire—
Abel learned this falling among the jellied
green creepers and morning-glories of the saurian sunset.
Stand still, you'll feel the sureness, the delirium,
rank and file certain of smashing the enemy,
Dundee's clans at Killiecrankie, who broke
the English, so three days later they were still running.
We're knotted together in innocence and guile;
yet we are not equal; I have lived without

sense so long the loss no longer hurts;
reflex and the ways of the world will float me free—
you, God help you, must will each breath you take.

3

Wishing to raise the cross of the Crucified King
in the monastery of Emmaus at Cuernavaca—
world names for their avant-garde crucifixes
and streamlined silver, the monks, like Paul, had earned
the cost of depth-transference by their craft.
A Papal Commission camped on them two years,
ruling analysis cannot be compulsory,
their cool Belgian prior was heretical, a fairy. . . .
We couldn't find the corpse removed by helicopter;
the cells were empty, but the art still sold;
lay-neurotics peeped out at you like deer,
barbwired in spotless whitewashed cabins, named
Sigmund and *Karl.* . . . They live the life of monks,
one revelation healing the ravage of the other.

4

The lizard rusty as a leaf rubbed rough
does nothing for days but puff his throat
for oxygen, and tongue up passing flies,
sees only similar rusty lizards pant:
harems worthy this lord of the universe—
each thing he does generic, and not the best.
How fragrantly our cold hands warm to the live coal!
We sit on the cliff like curs, chins pressed to thumbs,
the Toltec temples changing to dust in the dusk—
hair of the vulture, white brow of the moon: this too dust . . .
dust out of time, two clocks set back to the Toltec Eden,

as if we still wished to pull teeth with firetongs—
when they took a city, they too murdered everything:
man, woman and child, down to the pigs and dogs.

5

South of New England, south of Washington,
south of the South, I walk the glazed moonlight:
dew on the grass and nobody about . . .
drawn on by my unlimited desire,
like a bull with a ring in its nose and a chain in the ring. . . .
We moved far, bull and cow, could one imagine
cattle obliviously pairing for six long days:
up road and down, then up again this same
bricked garden road, stiff spines of hay stuck in our hides;
and always in full sight of everyone,
of the full sun, of the silhouetting sunset,
shown up by the undimmed lights of the passing car.
Then gone; I am learning to live in history.
What is history? What you cannot touch.

6

Midwinter in Mexico, yet the tall red flowers
stand up on many trees, and all's in leaf;
twilight bakes the wall-brick large as a loaf of bread—
somewhere I must have met this feverish pink before,
and knew its message; or is it that I walk
you home twenty times, and then turn back on my tracks?
No moment comes back to hand, not twice, not once.
We've waited, I think, a lifetime for this walk,
and the white powder beneath our feet slides out
like the sterile white salt of purity; even
your puffed lace blouse is salt. The bricks glide; the commonest

minute is not divided, not twice, not once. . . .
When you left, I thought of you each hour of the day,
each minute of the hour, each second of the minute.

7

Three pillows, end on end, and rolled in the daybed
blanket—elastic, curved and cool. For a second,
by some hallucination of the hand,
I thought I was unwrapping you. In the twilight,
the lavatory breathes out its sweet and shocking perfume,
Coca-Cola laced with rum. Dark, dear, dark:
here always, the night's illusory, houselights
watch Mexicans, mostly kids, squared up by boxlike
houses on a street where buses eat up the sidewalk.
And New Year's midnight: three in the market drink beer
from cans garnished with limes and salt; one woman, Aztec,
sings adultery ballads, and weeps because
her husband has left her for three women—to face
the poverty all men must face at the hour of death.

8

As if we chewed dry twigs and salt grasses,
filling our mouths with dust and bits of adobe,
lizards, rats and worms, we walk downhill,
love demanding we be calm, not lawful,
for laws imprison as much as they protect.
Six stone lions, hard drinkers, more like frogs,
guarding the fountain; three rusted arc-lights, rusting;
four stone inkfish, thrice stepped on, lifting the spout—
not starred in any guidebook . . . this city of the plain,
where the water turns red, as if it were dyed,
and thirteen girls sit at the barroom table,

then none, then only twenty coupled men,
homicidal with morality and lust—
devotion hikes uphill in iron shoes.

9

Looking about me with the strength of three,
three men, two women, or one unmarried, I see
the two immovable nuns, out of habit, too fat to leave
the dormitory, living for ten days on tea,
bouillon cubes, cookies bought and brought from Boston.
You curl in your metal bunk-bed like my child,
I sprawl at your elbow pillowed from the dead floor—
nuns packing, nuns ringing the circular iron stair,
nuns in pajamas scalloped through their wrappers,
nuns boiling bouillon, tea or cookies—nuns
brewing and blanketing reproval. . . .
The soul groans and laughs at its lack of stature—
if you want to make the frozen serpent dance,
you must sing it the music of its mouth.

10

No artist perhaps, you go beyond their phrases,
a girl too simple for this measured cunning. . . .
Take that day of baking on the marble veranda,
the roasting brown rock, the roasting brown grass, the breath
of the world risen like the ripe smoke of chestnuts,
a cleavage dropping miles to the valley's body;
and the following sick and thoughtful day
of the red flower, the hills, the valley, the Volcano—
this not the greatest thing, though great; the hours
of shivering, ache and burning, when we'd charged
so far beyond our courage—altitudes,

then the falling . . . falling back on honest speech:
infirmity, a food the flesh must swallow,
feeding our minds . . . the mind which is also flesh.

11

Sounds of a popping bonfire; no, a colleague's
early typing; or is he needing paregoric?
Poor Child, you were kissed so much you thought you were
    walked on;
yet you wait in my doorway with bluebells in your hair.
Those other yous, you think, are they meaningless in toto,
test-rockfalls you crudely approached and coarsely conquered,
leaving no juice in the flaw, mind lodged in mind?
Those others, those yous . . . a child wants everything—
things! A child, though earnest, is not quite mortal.
Love blots the categories; yet men trust
love's way is always through the common garden. . . .
I ask only coolness, stillness, intercourse—
sleep wastes the day lifelong behind your eyes,
night shivers at noonday in the boughs of the fir.

12

To clasp, not grasp the life and light and fragile;
as the intermeshing limbs of Lucifer
sink to sleep on the tumuli of Lilith. . . .
We're burnt, black chips knocked from the blackest stock:
Potato-famine Irish-Puritan, and Puritan—
gold made them smile like pigs once, then fear of falling—
hipbones finer than a breast of a squab,
eyes hard as stars, hearts small as elves, they turned
the wilderness to wood, then looked for trees.
They are still looking. Now our hesitant

conversation moves from lust to love;
friendship, without dissension, multiplying
days, days, days, days—how can I love you more,
short of turning into a criminal?

Canterbury

Regret those jousting aristocracies,
war-bright, though useless, their lives a round of games;
sex horsed their chivalry, even when
the aggressor was only an artless dragon. . . .
The Black Prince folds a missal in his hands,
rests, stone-chainmail, *imprimatur*, on his slab—
suppression hardened into gallantry;
behind the spasms of his ruffian hand,
slept a public school and sober faith in murder.
Here the worn pilgrim and kneeling savant ask:
'Do I have the right to imagination?'
Here the great fighter Captain lies with those
who made it, those whom fate disdained to wound.
All's dull here, all's peace here; theirs the new day.

Killiecrankie

The Scotch Lords once had means to salmon fish,
the painter means to paint them playing salmon,
gray crag, sunrise or sunset, brawling tarn,
poachers stripped, gashed, parceled to the birds—
if we do not fight, we had better break up and die.
In the Highlands, wherever war is not a science,
we humbly ask for nerve in our commander.
Ours kicked off the one pair of shoes in the clan
to walk us barefoot. The British drank the grass;
torrents of their redcoats and tartans raving down
the valley to the gorge of Killiecrankie.
Dundee's cuirass rose; still, he waved his sword,
he'd won the battle, lost his life and Scotland.
'If it's well with the King, it matters little to me.'

Midwinter

1 Friend across Central Park

Home from you, and through the trodden tangle,
the corny birdwalk, the pubescent knoll,
the dirtwood rowboats docked three deep, the tundra
between past Eightieth Street to Sixty-Seventh,
snow mucking to pepper and salt, to brain-cell dull,
to ink . . . to winter throwing off its decorations
on Manhattan, and on this day, in twenty minutes
inked from light to night—I thinking without pause
of you in Eisenhower's Washington,
I in my Dickensian muffler, snow-sugared, unraveling—
so you phantasized—in the waste thaw of loss:
winter and then a winter; unseared, your true voice seared,
still yearningly young; and I, though never young
in all our years, am younger when we meet.

2 Another Friend

Nothing less necessary than a girl shining a mirror,
waiting the miracle of the polishing winds,
mirrors turning dark to the leaf of May. . . .
You were not very wise, or unique in any skill;
not unreasonably, heaven became your enemy,
you knew your shadow to be the coming night;
knew from the steam of the straw the barn would burn.
I didn't want you to be warmed by walking,
each drop of perspiration on your face,
an admirer's eye. . . . Why do I remember
your galled young fingers painted with red ink,

that scar of an unfulfilled desire to be
the happiness of the drop to die in the river? . . .
The wave of the wineglass trembled to see you walk.

3 Judith

'The Latins are much like Arabs, as we say at Radcliffe;
decay of infeud scattered the Scottish clans,
but ours is an airier aristocracy:
professors, statesmen, new art, old, the city
where only Jews can write an English sentence,
the Jewish mother, half wasp, half anti-wasp,
says, *liberate, literate, liberalize*!
If her boy dies and takes his lay in state,
she calms the grandeur of his marble hair.
Like Judith, she would cut the Virgin Mary
or Marie-Antionette or Mary Stuart
leftist-Tsarists, jet-set parachutes;
knowing a lightweight is like knowing Holofernes—
smack! her sword divorced the codshead from the codspiece.'

4 Seal of the Fair Sex

'My mother's beau before I spoke to boys—
but *Uncle* Harold, now his eyes are going,
pops in here twice a week with country presents,
colorful, slightly corny garden truck,
his bounty to rich and poor since I was growing. . . .
Thirty raspberry bushes stacked on my sundeck,
set by himself in a long day doubled;
midrow, three plastic lilies, the everlastings,
paced for a grave—*for me to think of him,
when he lies uphill.* Do you find this amusing?'
'You are his crush, my Dear, he is in love;

when we are no more and dying, love is power.
Love, even in his hallucination, keeps. . . .'
'It's all that keeps off death at any time.'

5 The Goldfish

The biggest cat sees all through eyefilm, yawns
dreamily, 'Such a sweet young radical couple!'
She prays for the man to come without his wife.
The decks of windows graze on Central Park,
from such elevation the crowd is part of a movie,
and money flies in airmail to meet the rent.
'Is it as Marx dreamed, man is what he makes?'
She sighs. 'The rich have muscle.' The windows face
the unilluminating city lights,
as a goldfish might estimate the universe.
She sees the old left yielding place to new,
and eyes her guest, young, dissident, a trustee;
and tonight he is single, he has everything,
swims in her like an eel in the Bay of Fundy.

6 La Lumière

In the glaze of my glasses, you cannot alter—
ruffle, electricity and beak,
though wealthier now and much more radical. . . .
Sun enters the windows it has never crashed,
it is the blind snow, blind light everywhere,
the sad, metallic sunlight of New York
throwing a light on something about to die.
This light, familiar from former lives and cities,
discloses less than the leaves of an artichoke—
a twilight kind to kings who fled to London.
In this light Napoleon's Nephew looks like Dickens

cloaked in cigar smoke and the moans of girls,
the smell of chestnuts like a humidor . . .
watching exile chew his face from the mirror.

7 Elisabeth Schwarzkopf in New York

Yet people live here . . . Paris, Wien, Milano,
which had more genius, grace, preoccupations?
We pass up grace, our entrance fee and tithe
for dwelling in the heavenly Jerusalem—
small price for salience, and the world is here:
Elisabeth Schwarzkopf sings, herself her parts,
Wo ist Silvia and *die Marschallin*,
until the rivers of the early world,
the Hudson and the Tigris, burst their bar,
trembling like water-ivy down the spine,
from the satyr's tussock to his hardened hoof—
la Diva, crisped, remodeled for the boards,
roughs it with chaff and cardigan at recordings,
is anyone's single and useful weekend guest.

8 Across the Yard: La Ignota

The soprano's bosoms point to the joy of God,
Brunhild who would not rule her voice for God—
she has to sing to fill such windows, hang
such drapes: one is pink dust flipped back to scarlet,
the other besmirched gauze—behind the first,
a blown electric heater; behind the second,
and placed as furniture, her footlocker
with Munich stickers. No one really hires her;
her grandiose, arched wooden window frames
haven't felt paint or putty these twenty years;
grass, dead since Kennedy, chokes the window box.

Like a grackle, she flings her high aria through the trash. . . .
When I was lost and green, I would have given
the janitor three months' rent for this address.

School

1 For Peter Taylor

That doleful Kenyon snapshot: you ham-squat on your bed,
jaw hung sidewise, and your eyes too glossy;
chest syrup, wicked greens of diesel oil;
you the same sickly green, except you are
transparent. I can almost touch and smell
those pajamas we were too brush-off to change,
and wore as winter underwear through our trousers.
When the snapshot was developed, I saw you couldn't
live a week, and thought you might have died,
squatting upright, a last dynasty mummy.
You live on: earth's obliquities of health,
though Adams knew the Southerner must go under—
love teases. We're one still, we are weaker, wilder—
stuck in one room again, we want to fight.

2 Randall Jarrell

The dream went like a rake of sliced bamboo,
slats of the dust distracted by downdraw;
I woke and knew I held a cigarette;
I looked, there was none, could have been none;
I slept the years and I woke again,
palming the floor, shaking the sheets. I found
nothing smoking. I am awake, I see
the cigarette burn safely in my fingers. . . .
They come this path, old friends, old buffs of death.
Tonight it's Randall, the spark of fire though humbled,

his gnawed wrist cradled like his *Kitten*. 'What kept you so
   long,
racing your cooling grindstone to ambition?
Surely this life was fast enough. . . . But tell me,
Cal, why did we live? Why do we die?'

Lines from Israel

1 World War I, 1916

'I am beginning to rub my eyes at the prospect of peace,
when we will have to know the dead are not
dead only for the duration of the war;
I am in glowing looks, I've never seen
myself in such keen color, most by daylight. . . .
Strange to know suddenly in this slowly farewell war
that I know many more dead than I know living. . . .'
Turning the page in *Time* to see her picture,
expecting some London Judith, *no trespass,*
I touch your green shutter-sweater and breathing breasts:
Lady Cynthia Asquith, the undying bulwark of British girl. . . .
The word miracle was more common there than here,
yet sleeping with this one might not have been maneuvered—
each stone an acre, or unexploded minefield.

March, 1969

2 Sands of the Desert

The vagabond Alexander passed here, *romero*—
was he here in Israel, or in the Near East?
The province, still provincial, prays to the one God
who left his footmark on the field of blood;
its dry wind bleeds the overcharged barbed wire. . . .
And wherever the sun fermented man from dust,
our blood leaps up in friendship a cold spring. . . .
Alexander learned to share the earth with God;
God learned to live with heaven—a wizened distance,
his face a worsened sand-dollar on the pail of a child. . . .

117

Each year some prince of tyrants, King Ahab, says,
'If my enemies could only know me, I am safe.'
But the good murderer is always blind;
the leopard entered the Ark and keeps his spots.

3 Israel

These sidesteppings and obliquities, unable
to take the obvious truth on any subject:
three weeks in the sun of Israel . . . I might have stayed,
stayed and waited gladly to do service,
though almost a pacifist, and still not sure
the Arabs are black . . . no Jew, and thirty years
too worn. I loved the country, her briskness and freshness
jolting between salvation and demolition.
The way of Israel's god is military;
from X to X, the prophets, unto Marx—
reprisal and terror benumbed from voice to noise;
finally, no one tells us which is which—
till arms fuse and chemical reverts to desert,
semper idem et ubique, the God of Hosts.

Writers

1 T. S. Eliot

Caught between two streams of traffic, in the gloom
of Memorial Hall and Harvard's war-dead. . . . And he:
'Don't you loathe to be compared with your relatives?
I do. I've just found two of mine reviewed by Poe.
He wiped the floor with them . . . and I was *delighted*.'
Then on with warden's pace across the Yard,
talking of Pound, 'It's balls to say he only
pretends to be like Ezra. . . . He's better though. This year,
he no longer wants to rebuild the Temple at Jerusalem.
Yes, he's better. "*You* speak," he said, when he'd talked two
    hours.
By then I had absolutely nothing to *say*.'
Ah Tom, one muse, one music, had one the luck--
lost in the dark night of the brilliant talkers,
humor and honor from the everlasting dross!

2 Ezra Pound

Horizontal in a deckchair on the bleak ward,
some feeble-minded felon in pajamas, clawing
a Social Credit broadside from your table, you saying,
'. . . here with a black suit and black briefcase; in the briefcase,
an abomination, Possum's *hommage* to Milton.'
Then sprung; Rapallo, and then the decade gone;
then three years, then Eliot dead, you saying,
'And who is left to understand my jokes?
My old Brother in the arts . . . and besides, he was a smash of
    a poet.'

He showed us his blotched, bent hands, saying, 'Worms.
When I talked that nonsense about Jews on the Rome
wireless, she knew it was shit, and still loved me.'
And I, 'Who else has been in Purgatory?'
And he, 'To begin with a swelled head and end with swelled
   feet.'

3 Ford Madox Ford

Taking in longhand Ford's dictation on Provence,
the great Prosateur swallowing his Yorkshire British,
I fishing for what he said each second sentence—
'You have no ear,' he said, 'for the Lord's prose,
Shakespeare's medium: *No king, be his cause never so spotless,*
will try it out with all unspotted soldiers.'
I brought him my loaded and overloaded lines.
He said, 'You have your butterfly existence:
half hour of work, two minutes to love, the rest boredom.
Conrad spent a day finding the *mot juste*; then killed it.'
In time, he thought, I might live to be an artist.
'Most of them are born to fill the graveyards.'
'If he fails as a writer,' Ford wrote my father, 'at least
he'll be Ambassador to England, or President of Harvard.'

4 To Allen Tate I

My longest drive, two hundred miles, it seemed:
Nashville to Clarksville to the Cumberland River,
March 1937, in *my* month Pisces,
Europe's last fling of impotence and anger—
and above your fire the blood-crossed flag of the States,
a Stonewall Jackson, a twenty-two at half-cock—
you routing the windmills with only a gamecock's warcries.
And the moonshine was as white as water;

tall, dirty, stately setpieces in Southern patois;
saying your tenant with ten children had more art
than Thomas Wolfe. And, 'Do they expect me to leave the
    South
to meet frivolous people like Tugwell and Mrs. Roosevelt?'
Ford, playing Russian Banker in that half-light, sneering,
'You must show your cards, dear Tate . . . it isn't done.'

5 *To Allen Tate II*

On your enormous brow, cannonball head of a snowman,
is a ripped red tissuepaper birthday hat;
you squint, make out my daughter, then six or seven:
'*You* are a Southern *belle*; do you know why
you are a *Southern* belle?' (Stares, stupor, thumb in her mouth)
'Because your *mother* is a Southern belle.'
Your attention wanders, 'I love you now, but I'll love you
more probably when you are older.' Harriet whispering,
'If you are still alive.' We reach Gettysburg;
both of us too much the soldier from Sourmash:
'I don't know whether to call you my son or my brother.'
Ashtrays and icecubes deployed as Pickett's columns:
a sloping forest of flashing steel. You point:
'There, if Longstreet had *moved*, we would have *broke* you.'

6 *William Carlos Williams*

Whom would I love more? William Carlos Williams,
in collegiate black slacks, gabardine coat,
and loafers polished like the rosewood on yachts,
straying stonefoot through his town-end garden,
man and flower seedy with three autumn strokes,
his brown, horned eyes enlarged, an ant's, through glasses;
his Mother, stonedeaf, her face a wrinkled talon,

burnt-out ash of her long-haired Puerto Rican grasses;
the black, blind, bituminous eye is inquisitorial.
'Mama,' he says, 'which would you rather see here,
us or three blondes?' Then later, 'The old bitches
live into their hundreds, while I'll kick off tomorrow.'
And saying, 'I am sixty-seven, and more
attractive to girls than when I was seventeen.'

7 Robert Frost

Robert Frost at midnight, the audience gone
to vapor, the great act laid on the shelf in mothballs,
his voice musical, raw and raw—he writes in the flyleaf:
'Robert Lowell from Robert Frost, his friend in the art.'
'Sometimes I feel too full of myself,' I say.
And he, misunderstanding, 'When I am low,
I stray away. My son wasn't your kind. The night
we told him Merrill Moore would come to treat him,
he said, "I'll kill him first." One of my daughters thought
    things,
knew every male she met was out to make her;
the way she dresses, she couldn't make a whorehouse.'
And I, 'Sometimes I'm so happy I can't stand myself.'
And he, 'When I am too full of joy, I think
how little good my health did anyone near me.'

Those Older

1

They won't stay gone, rising with royal torpor,
as if held in my binoculars' fog and enlargement,
casting the raindrops of the rainbow: children;
loved by their still older elders in a springtide
invisible to us as the Hittites. We're too near now
to date their comings and goings—those *late* people:
Cousin Susie and Cousin Belle. Fate stamped
them with their maiden name *for life*—blood-rich,
and constellations from the dancing heart.
Our first to die . . . so odd and light and dry,
they seemed foreshadows of some earlier, strange creation,
hooded in snail-shells, the unassailable
deafness of their formidable asperity—
our girls . . . less than a toy, and more than a flower.

2

Another was a man who lived the middle life
from the days of his youth till the day of his death;
and yet the matching of his fresh-cut flowers
was over-delicate and dead for death,
as if the flowery coverlet lay like lead,
asserting that no primitive ferment
or slobbering poignance of the voyeur God
would ever corrupt or soil his earthly vestment
spread like King Solomon in the Episcopal morgue,
sanguine, still patient with his thousand lovers. . . .
Here at world's end, here with nowhere else to go,

lie those before us, and those just before us:
less than a toy, and more than a flower . . .
rich and poor, the poor . . . no trees in the sky.

3

No fence stands up between us and our object:
approaching nearer, edging out the old,
and free to pick those neither ripe nor young,
as the hollow green wilderness sings the guillotine,
sings those before us. . . . I have had them fifty years:
all those grander, or finer, or simply older,
gone astraying down a backward street, the trees,
late-lopped, tar-boned, old prunes like stumps of martyrs;
and even this dead timber is bulldozed rootless,
and we face faceless lines of white frame houses,
sanded, stranded, undarkened by shade or shutter—
rich and poor . . . no trees in the sky—their stones,
so close they melt to a field of snow, if we pass,
won from the least desire to have what is.

Death

(FOR I. A. RICHARDS)

Our one intimate metaphysical—
sooner or later, death looks fair on all,
its look, pale primrose with blood-drinking sighs. . . .
Or Ivor Richards talking to this subject,
'My vanity won't let me believe my death.'
In this generous world-time, ought but vanity,
sleep never catches up with those God speeds—
so much we wished our world's eternity. . . .
'A suicide takes chances. I'd choose the ocean,
who knows, I might reach the other side.
If the coin flips, I'll see the other side.'
Hob-Alpine Spirit, you saved so much illusion
by changing its false coin to words . . . all high,
blind from bright heights, foreseeing you were air.

Ice on the Hudson

1

The air is snow-touched, fans our streaming backs,
blows in and in, a thousand snow-years back;
we were joined in love a thousand snow-years back.
Snow purifies the air that breathes our flesh,
waterfall white of China flays the glass;
but this is dream, no storm dare set a foot in,
blown spray nor wave can reach our stilted window.
Will the white foam-wisp soil with poison when it hits
the Hudson's prone and essence-steaming back,
the Great Arriviste in the metropolis?
Manhattan is pierced by the stiletto heel—
this too a dream; New York was never a person. . . .
In the days of the freeze, we see a minor sun,
our winter moon bled for the solar rose.

2

They too have had their saints and Roundhead cells
to guide them down the narrow path and true,
home to desolation and regimental terror—
policemen martyrs . . . theirs was something of an artist
at his vague, dreamlike trade of blood and guile—
one joke meant death—meat stuck between that tooth
and gum began to stink in half a second. . . .
Ah the rain rains down in drops like iron balls;
the River's ice-jammed; miserable Manhattan
stands on stilts to the taunts of black ice heaven.
O when will we sleep out the storm, dear love,

say to the minute, stop for good, stop dead,
see at the end of our walk some girl's burnt-yellow legs
glow, as if she had absorbed the sun?

Chairs

The big frog fits the soft chair of the master,
ink licked from the warts and creases of his skin,
vapor of venom and commonplace and joy.
Whenever he croaks, a rival has to plunge;
no flattery warms the slime of the sadist,
feared and nondescript on his green pad.
His girl with a taperecorder has total recall. . . .
Wars have silenced half the classic tongues,
France died on the motionless lines of Marshal Joffre;
something went better, in the last parades,
we marched from present safety to future menace. . . .
New men of letters leap like frogs in the spring,
sports in the youthful green of pliant sheen—
scratching each other's backs like cans in a sack.

My Death

1

Reading this book to four or five that night
at Cuernavaca, till the lines glowered and glowed,
and my friend, Monsignor Illich, ascetic donkey,
braying, 'Will you die, when the book is done?'
It stopped my heart, and not my mouth. I said,
'I have begun to wonder.' Lapsed R.C.
caught mid journey to atheist, I knew
I must pay for this opportunist violation.
Or was his *die: as if,* his gracenote saying,
'It is writing, if you run, as if to die.'
Christ's first portrait is a donkey's head,
the simple truth is in his simple word,
lies buried in a random, haggard sentence,
cutting ten ways to nothing clearly carried.

2

The dream is changing costume, set and cast,
all working more in character than life—
It is a sort of Harvard of the arts,
though none I met were artists, only people.
At the top of hightable, I heighten my jokes, and shake
salt on the winespots, till I sit alone,
talking to someone presently my father.
His hair, grown richer, peacocks out in bangs;
'I do it,' he says, 'to look manlier and younger.
I have had to sink all my spare money in courses:
calc and singing, and my trusty math.'

We were joined in the arts, though old. Then I,
'I have never loved you so much in all our lives.'
And he, 'Doesn't it begin at the beginning?'

February and March

1 Cows

The cows of Potter and Albert Cuyp are timeless;
in the depths of Europe, we find their scrawly pastures
and scrawlier hamlets unwatered by paint or Hegel,
the benighted provincial kirk. None of our rear-guard painters,
the lover of nature, the hater of abstraction,
can do these landscapes. With a bull's watery eye,
dewlap and misty phallus, Cuyp caught the farthest glisten,
tonnage and rumination of the sod. . . .
And there is a whiteness; behind your sixties dress,
feudal vassal's workday, and R.C. code,
lies the windfall abandon of Giorgione,
Renaissance idleness—only the lovely,
the good, the wealthy served the Venetian, whose art
knew nothing yet of husbandry and cattle.

2 The Golden Middle

The ceiling is twenty feet above our heads;
oak panels, mantel and oak linoleum tiles;
book-ladders on brass rods and rollers touch the sky—
in middle age, the good costs less and less. . . .
Who can deduct these years? Become a student,
graced with rebellion, hair and the caw of Shelley,
his hectic hopes, his tremulous success,
the ignominious and bitter death?
Here the hard, cunning light would leave his eyes,
soon he would starve his genius for denial,
hear a song in the pipes, the chirp of frogs,

and turn with the tread of an ox to serve the rich,
clinging to status, police and private schools
to lift their feet from the mud of the republic.

3 Father's Album

These well-planned dinner parties, wife and husband,
no passengers were senior to my parents,
rank won at the captain's table one day at sea—
INDISPENSABLE . . . like Franklin Roosevelt,
dying and solar on his fourth campaign—
coming to power by reaching public opinion,
cementing public opinion by use of power.
He used time; time was his servant not his master. . . .
You learn to be yourself; at first it's freedom,
and then paralysis, then you are yourself—
in the face of the world's most powerful army,
they snatched their third of a million men from Belgium;
for the first time England was spiritually in the war,
the move, like so many British retreats, a triumph.

4 Vigil

Famine's joy is in the enjoyment; who'll deny
the crash, delirious uterus living it up?
Therefore, we lie here, in heat or cold—heat knocking,
winter brushing the window white with frost.
It's not good moments, but the town defruited
gives us the toothache . . . to destroy a people
for its own good, and let the world go by:
green year, a green year, twenty percent for peace,
now down to ten or nine. We breathe, we live,
since our death is useless to killed or killing,
since the window shatters and the wind is blowing,

since the trees are leafless and the boughs are green,
the hunters hunted. . . . Why do we live and breathe—
tough as the cat, nine lives to go, then none?

5 Le Cygne

The virgin, the blind, the beautiful today,
dares it break the mirror of this lake,
hard, neglectful, hoarding under ice
a great glacier of flights that never fly?
The swan worsens, remembers it is he,
the magnificence that gives itself no hope,
the fortitude that finds no *raison d'être*—
the great boredoms blaze in the sterile winter.
The whole neck shakes in this white agony
inflicted by the space the swan denies;
he cannot deny the ice that ties his feet.
His pure brilliance led him to this grand asylum,
governed by staccato cries of grandeur,
pride that clothes the swan in useless exile.

6 Thirst

We have taken too much salt here—thirst without
bottom; young we dug acid from the saltmarsh;
your hand, a small monkey's, cannot scratch our names;
the chilling glass of julep blows to pollen.
There'll be no more. Some can escape in sleep;
they find their tunnel, and its only exit,
a hole soon filled with twenty slides of rock;
the oxygen expires; we hope the wind will rush
through a smashed window, that Faith will move the moun-
tain.
Who has met death with warmth? I know, it's like that:

in love, forgetting. Few are able to love,
bear their bearers, the never to be forgotten
my father, *my* mother . . . these names, this function, given
by them once, given existence now by us.

7 *The Human Race*

One cushion is the seat and back of the creaky chair,
is a full green leaf; the four walls, ceiling, hinges, locks,
eerie asylum green on blueglow—I know,
I am here, they never let me finish a sentence. . . .
Taxi drivers always hold the floor;
born with direction, crackling a roll of bills,
buying any juice that burns—the hacks,
unerring, sentenced to live in a world of fools,
how many voyagers have they talked to death—
in forts of gunproof plastic, swift as Achilles,
they daily run their course to the edge of the void. . . .
Green leaf, green walls. I walk from wall to wall;
taxis dissect New York . . . one, unable
to see he is finished, goes on into the wall.

8 *Helltime*

Our God; he walks with us, he talks with us,
in sleep, in thunder, and in wind and weather;
he strips the wind and gravel from our words,
and speeds us naked on the single way.
Is he wind, or is he revelation,
the time-bomb buried in this ton of trash?
In some Bolivian tin mine we, the servants,
drop-outs and hoop-spines sway the cart together;
God finds no profit in descending here,
finds only smear, expendables of love,

nothing and helltime borne by faithful servants,
you have your place . . . if you are put
in your place enough times, you become your place . . .
the flatterer's all-forgiving, wounded smile.

9 *Under the Screw*

—I don't care if she wants to lay the Negro,
it's hearing her lush it out in company. . . .
—Why you worry if your Half don't worry?
—She can fry Harlem for breakfast, I don't broadcast. . . .
In our set, God is an entirely lost person—
there were two: Benito Mussolini and Hitler,
blind mouths shouting people into things.
After their Chicago deaths with girls and gunshot,
who'll say they gave a fresh plot to what they planned?
No league against the ephemeral Enemy lasts;
not even the old aristocracy of the Commune
curing the seven plagues of economics,
to wither daily in favor of the state,
covenant of swords without the word.

10 *Oversleeping*

This glorious oversleeping into Sunday,
the sickroom's crimeless mortuary calm,
celestial arrows hitting the drawn drape;
though we are city, light goes up to heaven,
a better world, Utopia far beyond
the bicker of abstracts, the Bomb's farsighted vigil.
I pity the sprained rightness of the boy,
his color-blind vision showing gray,
when a third of the globe was colored red for Britain. . . .
Let us have peace, house-peace, peace in New York,

peace instead of pace, or the Sunday paper,
black with dirtsores, the loneliness of children,
the reader's need as reader to think these beings
made for suffering should suffer well.

11 In the Family

One doubts the wisdom of almighty God
casting weak husbands adrift in the hands of a wife.
We jangle like fishwives. Our hopes are more disputed
than our quarrels. Love lives on trial
like the Carlyles fighting meat from the mouth of their dog.
Lucky the Carlyles couldn't bear children;
ours, has me, 'Genius, unwise, unbrilliant, weird,'
has you, 'Brilliant, unwise, unweird, nerves.'
Barbaric cheek is needed to stay married,
imagination weds the hand of the writer to types—
Lizzie, we wake up to the blood of loneliness,
we would cry out *Love, Love,* if we had letters.
We are all here for such a short time,
we might as well be good to one another.

12 Left out of Vacation

'Some fathers may have some consideration,
but he is so wonderfully eccentric,
drinking buttermilk and wearing red socks.
It was OK—not having him in Florida;
Florence is different, Mother—big deal, two girls
alone in the Italian restaurant!' . . .
Only our God could destroy the wonders He made,
and shelve you too among them, Charles Sumner Lowell,
shiny horsechestnut-colored Burmese Cat,
swaying your haunches like a literary lion,

our animal whose only friends are persons—
now boarded with cats in a cat-house, moved at random
by the universal Love that moves the stars
rehearsing forever the perfected comeback.

13 *Red and Black Brick Boston*

My time will not extend, though I want love;
light takes on meaning any afternoon
now, or ten years forward, or anywhere.
The sun baking the red and black brick red,
the red glow made by art and LSD,
or the sun that shines on something worthy,
imitating visible eternity.
Eternity isn't love, or absolution
a man or a woman yoked in love though married
and risking their souls to snatch a child's attention. . . .
I am distracted by the soiled red brick,
my senseless originality for fact,
red brick, once cheap, and boastful, 'Boston is,
Rome was.' A good confession should end in prayer.

14 *Utopia for Racoons*

My goiter expert smiles like a racoon,
'O.K., you're rich and can afford to die.'
Claws me a minute, claws his notes for five,
claws me a day, then claws the notes for five;
could crack an adam's-apple like a walnut.
The doctor washes, licks his paws of me,
and sips his fountainpen for bubbly ink.
On a second floor in a second hospital,
two racoons wear stethoscopes to count the pulse
of their geiger-counter and their thyroid scan;

they sit sipping my radioactive iodine
from a small lead bottle with two metal straws,
'What little health we have is stolen fruit.
What is the life-expectancy of a racoon?'

15 Under the Dentist

'When I say you *feel*, I mean you *don't*. This thing's
metaphysical not sensitive:
you come here in your state of hypertension.
Bob . . . you lie quiet, you are very good,
you can feel the jangling in your nerves,
you will feel the city jangling in your nerves,
a professor might even feel the cosmos jangling.
If you read news, news jangles in your hands.
You don't have to be I.Q. or a reporter
to have feelings. Thinking burns out nerve;
that's why you cub professors calcify.
You got brains, why do you smoke? I stopped smoking,
    drinking,
not pussy . . . it's not vice. I drill here 8 to 5,
make New York in the sunrise—I've got nerves.'

16 Sense of Reality

We never see him now, except at dinner,
then you quarrel, and he goes upstairs. . . .
My old playground keeps its asphalt base:
no growth, two broken swings, the well one—as was!
Our half century fought, and held.
The eye's a liar, the precinct has turned hard,
hard more like a person than a thing,
time that mends most objects leaves men free,
no doctor does the job of the carpenter.

It's the ideology dies first—then you, Dear,
so used, worn out, thumbed, got by heart, praised, painted;
or I, contracted to a juster perspective,
fired by my second alcohol, remorse,
doing all for the best, and therefore doing nothing.

17 Fame

We bleed for people, so independent and selfsuspicious,
if the door is locked, they just come back, instead of knock-
    ing—
hearts scarred by complaints they would not advance;
it was not their good fortune to meet their love;
however long they lived, they would still be waiting.
We believed you, they said, by believing you were lying. . . .
Timur saying something like: 'The drop of water
that fails to become a river is food for the dust.
The eye that cannot size up the whole of the Tigris
in a drop is an acorn, not the eye of a man. . . .'
His face in the mirror was like the sun on a dewdrop;
the path to death was always underfoot;
this the sum of the world's scattered elements—
fame, a bouquet in the niche of forgetfulness!

18 Growing in Favor

This waking with a start of pathos to fear—
it comes too often now, though no less often
in the year of my first razor and the death of God;
thick then my tongue, as if anesthetized,
the silkscreen fish gaped air into a bubble,
the wallflower drank dank plaster, turned a cabbage,
the feeble household pump sighed on its block. . . .
A little further on, and I am nature:

139

my pinch of dust lies on the eternal dust-tray,
lies on call forever, never called. . . .
Who will call for me, call girl, when I start awake,
all my diminishment retarded, wake
to sing the dawnless alba of the gerontoi? . . .
Old age is all right, but it has no future.

19 Keepsakes: A Dead Letter

'If once a winter with absent heart, you look,
then push the ingots underneath the checkstubs—
dating children with trash was your strong suit. . . .
These are not rape, but things for Lost and Found:
stage garnet, Spick-coin, bronze boss, thin true gold chain,
its ABC design too intricate
for the child to spell. Can you still spell my name?
Do you whisper, "Mine rich with senseless power—"
won by man's turbulant, pretentious meekness,
my gloating willingness for the sullen delight?
Has excessive skating cracked the ice? Do you still
swell your stomach with oracle, "Girls make things happen,"
though you fear to idle too much energy
in first-hand exercise of this religion?'

20 Last Summer

Asleep just now, just now I am awake,
see a man designed on the back of a card:
his trousers, laundered green; his coat, wet leaf;
his fair young flesh, sky-green of the deep vein.
I turn the card, the figure is trees and grass—
last summer for the wondered mind . . . for seeing
the dead servant's green turf beyond the pale,
white marble mantel, bust, rolled rug, the sheeted den,

the old master covered with his pillowslip—
searching as everyman for my one good deed,
crying love lost in the long apprenticeship:
friend, wife or child, their vanished art of breathing;
knowing I must forget how to breathe through my mouth,
now I am dead, and just now I was made.

21 Cranach's Man-Hunt

Composed, you will say, for our ever friendship,
almost one arm around our many shoulders,
one shade darkens the stream of the photograph,
friends bound by birth and accent . . . we had one.
We're game for the deer-hunt, ages five to ninety,
seniority no cipher to who will die
on this clearing of blown, tame grass, a trap of landscape,
green bow in the bend of the choppy, lavender stream,
eighteen or nineteen of us, bounding or swimming,
hurt stags and does . . . the Kaiser Maximilian
and the wise Saxon Elector, screened by one clump,
winching their crossbows . . . the horsemen, picadors,
whipped to action by their beautiful, verminous dogs,
to this battle the Prince has never renounced or lost.

22 Death and the Bridge
(*From a Landscape by Frank Parker*)

Death gallops up the bridge of red railtie girders,
some onetime view of Boston humps the saltmarsh;
it is handpainted: this the eternal, provincial
city Dante saw as Florence and hell. . . .
On weekends too, the local TV station's
garbage disposal starts to grind at daybreak:
keep Sunday clean. We owe the Lord that much;

from the first, God heeded His socialistic conscience,
gave universal capital punishment.
In daylight, the relaxed red scaffolding is almost
breathing: *no man is ever too good to die*. . . .
We will follow our skeletons on the girder,
out of life and Boston, singing with Freud:
'God's ways are dark and very seldom pleasant.'

23 First Spring

Its gloom is fertile, I almost breathe-in rain
horseclopping down from fire-escape to skylight
to dungeon courtyard; the rain renews. Not here,
till spring, till the snakehead breaks the yielding crust;
a smell, not taste, of life. For whom? For what?
For the horses, six bets in ten misplaced,
when another younger generation faces
the firing squad and our blood is wiped from the pavement.
For our passive courage, paralysis
that held us upright like tenpins to face the strike—
Coleridge's laudanum and brandy,
his alderman's stroll to positive negation—
his large plant with pith within, not heart of wood,
power without strength, an involuntary impostor.

24 Dear Sorrow

(FOR ELIZABETH)

We are over-ripened fruit, the soil of the earth;
justice is strife, and war the father of gods.
We go to the last, and not to last—
clock days swallowing letters, mouth and bed,
the open window roughing the central heat,
our Audubon *Bluejays* and *Sir Thomas More*,

142

the city with more sounds than the woodsman knew.
Our love will not come back on fortune's wheel;
this room will dim and die as we dim and die
to the many things . . . are the many things.
I beseech forgiveness from my wife and child . . .
my life spent in lifework—soul
cannot be saved outside the rôle of God,
man in the world like the whirlpool in a river.

25 Rembrandt

His faces crack . . . if mine could crack and breathe!
His Jewish Bridegroom, palm spread on the Jewish Bride's
bashful, taffeta-leveled bosom, is faithful;
the fair girl, poor background, gives soul to his flayed steer.
Her breasts, the snowdrop, last into the storm;
often the Dutch were sacks, their women a sack,
obstinate, undefeated hull of the old scow.
But Bathsheba's ample stomach, her heavy, practical feet,
are reverently dried by the faithful servant,
his eyes dwell lovingly on each fulfilled sag;
her unfortunate body is the privilege of his service,
loose radiance of his spirit void of possession. . . .
One sees, if one sees at all, through a red mist
the strange new idol of the marketplace.

Pastime

1

Unorthodox sleep in the active hour:
young afternoon, the room, half-darkened, is day,
the raw draft brushing sock and soul.
Like cells of a charging battery, I charge up sleep—
if such sleep lasts, I touch eternity.
This, its pulse-stop, must have been before.
What is true is not real: I here, this bed here, this hour here,
mid-day inscrutable behind these blinds.
When truth says goodmorning, it means goodbye.
Voices drop from forms of distant apartments,
voices of schoolboys . . . they are always ours,
early prep-school; just as this hour is always
optional recess—this has been before:
the sting of touching past time by dropping off.

2

Labor to pull the raw breath through my closed nostrils
brings back breathing another, rawer air,
drawn freely enough from ice-crust football,
sunlight gilding the golden polo coats
of boys with country seats on the Dutch Hudson.
But why does that light stay? First Form football,
first time being sent on errands by a schoolmate—
Bobby Delano, cousin of Franklin Delano Roosevelt,
escorted drunk off the Presidential yacht,
winner of the football and hockey letters at fifteen;
at fifteen, expelled. He dug my ass with a compass,

and forced me to say my mother was a whore.
My freshman year, he shot himself in Rio,
odious, unknowable, inspired as Ajax.

April 8, 1968

1 Two Walls

Somewhere a white wall faces a white wall,
one wakes the other, the other wakes the first,
each burning in the other's borrowed splendor—
the walls, once woken, are forced to go on talking,
their color looks much alike, two shadings of white,
each living in the shadow of the other.
How fine these distinctions when we cannot choose!
Don Giovanni must have drawn sword on such an avenger,
two contracting, white stone walls—their pursuit
of happiness and his, coincident. . . .
At this point of civilization, this point of the world,
the only satisfactory companion we
can imagine is death—this morning, skin lumping in my
   throat,
I lie here, heavily breathing, the soul of New York.

2 Words of a Young Girl

'The broom trees twirped by our rosewood bungalow,
not wildlife, these were tropical and straw;
the Gulf fell like a shower on the fiber-sand;
it wasn't ocean like our Maine coast,
on ice for summer. We met a couple, not people,
squares asking Father whether he was his name—
none ever said that I was Harriet.
They were laying a beach-fire, and the sticks were guns;
our little bungalow was burning—it
had burned and we were in it, yet the guns

were only firecrackers made of scarlet cardboard;
the shots were boom, the fire was fizz. . . . Months later,
we scrubbed away our scars and blisters, unable
to answer if we had ever hurt.'

3 Petit Bourgeois

Our floor, ganged, liberated, not yet fire—
hand over hand on the one knotted rope, the boy,
a cool crew haircut, tans above the ledge,
smiling at me to mount his shoulders, swing
down fifty tiers of windows, two city blocks,
on that frail thread, that singed and swinging rope,
our building from here, a tapered, swaying rope,
fat head and narrow base—Louis Philippe's
face mirrored pear-shaped in a silver spoon.
You must go down the rope to save your life;
long ago, this was answered by hallucination:
if forced to walk to safety on a tightrope,
if my life swung on my will and skill . . . better to die.
The crowds in the street were cheering, when we refused.

Mania

1 1958

Remember standing with me in the dark,
Ann Adden? In the wild house? Everything—
I mad, you mad for me? And brought my ring,
that twelve-carat lunk of gold there . . . my Joan of Arc,
undeviating then from the true mark—
robust, ah taciturn! Remember our playing
Marian Anderson in Mozart's *Shepherd King*,
Il Re Pastore there? O Hammerheaded Shark,
the Rainbow Salmon of the World, your hand
a rose—not there, a week earlier! We stand. . . .
We ski-walked the eggshell at the Mittersill,
Pascal's infinite, perfect, fearful sphere—
the border nowhere, your center everywhere. . . .
And if I forget you, Ann, may my right hand. . . .

2 Heidegger

'Have you ever lost a year off . . . somewhere?
The new owner can't sell it back to us, can he?
Our terrible losses, Harry Truman's loss
of a minute's sleep for Hiroshima, less than
a boy catching the paw of his mutt in the door of a car. . . .
We're ghosts. . . . Twice I heard a rattling stress of cherry-
     stones,
then by my bed, a man. That flight was feudal
on steel-capped hoof and wing and foot of blood.
I've killed worse dragons—my doctor's thesis on Heidegger
in German, in Germany, for my German Prof,

I love Lenin, he was so feudal. "When I listen to Beethoven,"
he said, "I think of stroking people's hair;
what we need are people to chop the head off."
That horizontal is blood-colored and made by man.'

3 1968

'Dear Lowell, sitting sixty feet above the sea,
hearing my father build a house on this cliff,
sixty feet above the Penobscot Bay,
returning here from my ten years in Europe,
waiting for emigration papers, work cards etc.;
I chanced to read your book, *Near the Ocean*.
We're older . . . an extending potency. . . .
What I'd like to say is humanity,
like the black pharaohs the first Egyptians sculpted.
What I write to tell you is what a shining
remembrance of someone, of you, to hold of . . . me—
I aggrandize. . . . *1958;* now thundered
all the way through to that seemingly virginal time,
I fled America. We have a Viking son of three.'

Mania in Buenos Aires 1962

At the Hotel Continental, always
I heard the bulky, beefy, breathing herd.
Cow clothes. My coat limp chestnut-colored suede
cut to match my point shoes that hurt my toes.
That day cast a light of the next world. The bellow
of Juan Peron, the nymphets' Don Giovanni;
the good air; the *places*; the frowning starch-collared crowds—
Coups of the leaden internecine soldier,
Lumps of dough on the chessboard. . . . By sunlit cypress,
the Republican martyrs lie in Roman temples,
Man and goddess, busts of a rebel middleclass
still pale from the great kiss of Liberty. . . .
All night till my shoes were bloody I found rest
cupping my soft palm to her stone breast.

April

1 Roulette

Didn't Plato ban philosopher-professors,
the idols of the young, from the Republic?
And hardshell republicans? It wasn't just
the artist. The Republic! But it never was,
except in the sky-ether of Plato's thought,
steam from the ordure of his city-state.
His roulette wheel repeats; the man in the street
is mobile—never since Adam delved, such plans,
Utopia dimmed before the blueprint dries.
This much still certain: whoever takes the sword
must die by the sword, or someone else will die;
it doesn't matter—injustice slays disorder—
it doesn't matter, new establishments
will serve the people, the people people serve.

2 Europa

The headache, the night of no performance, duskbreak:
limping home by the fountain's Dionysiac gushes,
water smote from marble, the felon water,
the watery alcoholic going underground
to the stone museum. . . . We were an empire, soul-brothers
to Babylon and China, their imperishable
hope to go beyond the growth of hope.
In the dark night of lust's defensive backstep,
your breasts were breathing—like your will to breathe;
we should have bred *in aeternum*, instead of doing nothing.
Am I your only lover who never died?

I watch your breasts, white bull's eyes cupped by tan,
flatten on the leather and horn of Jupiter,
daring to raise his privates to the Godhead.

3 Redskin

Unsheathed, you unexpectedly go redskin,
except for two white torches, fruits of summer,
woman's headlights to guide us to the dark,
love of the body, the only love man is.
Woman looks natural in herself, not man,
equipped with his redemptive bat and balls—
Renoir, paralyzed, painted with his penis,
did naked women, not Michelangelos.
Rain claws the door, a thousand fingernails;
your icy, poorly circulating fingers
trickle all night from heaven to the skin;
they will be warm by day, and we be warm—
at wrath-break, when the earth and ocean merge,
who wants to hold his weapon to the whale?

4 Dalliance

All was respectability, pleasant and dark;
dalliance means to dwell the hour with Eros—
this flower I take away and wear with fear,
who will notice? Othello never caught
Cassio reeking Desdemona's musk.
You grow more comforting as you excite,
like the Macbeth murk of Manhattan in sunset smog.
Others dragged back to Manhattan . . . Herman Melville
set at the helm, facing a pot of coals,
the sleet and wind spinning him ninety degrees,
'I must not give me up then to the fire,

lest it invert my fire; it blinded me,
so did it me. . . . There's a wisdom that is woe,
but there is a woe that is madness.'

5 Dialogue

'One's family meetings in what new foreign bar?
Which lover is one's mother with this week?
Peers, bel Antonios, pilots, her great men,
almost by definition, were the jocks;
bantering insolence puffed the ponderous pigskin—
charging, they did not cheer or shout; they growled. . . .
'When I sought fame in my youth, I little knew
how near the catch was: books and vanity,
vast womb of echoes bound by injured nerve. . . .
I kept my ambitions leashed and only read
to one or two friends.' 'You found a million friends.
In this short, indefinite time, I'll marry the least man,
the top of whose husbandry is raising flowers—
no sense in shouting the truth from the wrong window.'

6 The Misanthrope and the Painter

'The misanthrope: a woman who hates man.
Women are stronger, but we are smarter.' 'Mostly
woman hates his drinking and his women,
hates this in all men; she will not permit
Cassio to step into Othello's shoes.'
'Listen to the artist on her fellow artist,
a woman on a woman.' 'The only way Sue can
repaint this one is throw herself under a truck.'
'I pick up lines from nothing.' 'I'm not nothing, Baby;
when I'm in a room, Wyeth is invisible.'
'When Rembrandt had painted the last red spot on the nose

of a clown or Rembrandt, he disappeared in the paint.
I pick lines from the trash.' 'I'm not garbage, Baby.
You may have *joie de vivre*, but you're not twenty.'

7 Even Such

'One step, two steps, one step, two steps, one step—
time takes our youth, our joys and all we have;
its First Commandment is to keep the step,
the Second Commandment is like it. A noble nature
has no alarmclock but the almanac;
throws out the clocks and navigates by star.'
'Christ might have lived forever, if he'd lived
from sun to sun, and kept a twelve-hour night.'
'I know a too healthy sleep foreshadows death.'
'Did anyone ever sleep with anyone
without thinking a split second he was God?'
'Even if such a one indiscreetly writes
the perfect sentence, he knows it isn't English;
he goes to bed Lord Byron, but wakes up bald.'

8 The White Goddess

'I'm scratchy, I don't wear these epaulets
tacked to my chest for you to lift and pose. . . .
As girls, we used to moon on the Amazons;
after our ten hour treks, we snorted ten hours
or more, we had to let our souls catch up—
men will never, we thought, come up to women. . . .
Later on the floodlit stage of the *Opera*,
my Goddess was the Gold Coast Black singing
Verdi's *Desdemona* to the ebbing gold.
She took *Otello*, died, took her bow. She said,
with noble shyness, "I appreciate

your cooperation with my shortcomings . . .
I wish on you the love of God, and a friend,
who never met the woman she couldn't make." '

9 Topless

If breast-feeding is servile and for the mammals,
the best breasts in the nightclub are fossils—
single men can't go nearer than the bar;
by listing, I feel the rotations of her breeze;
dancing, she flickers like the family hearth.
I gaze on the old foundations of western marriage,
as if I were looking at a work of art,
and not the one thing necessary most husbands
have resigned and want. She is the girl,
as Renoir, Titian and all full times have left her,
no victim to strict diet, but its fulfilment—
chicken turtle climbing up the glass,
managing her invertebrae like hands,
lug-tits of man's crash-love, and her affliction.

10 A Souvenir

Between 6 and 7 A.M. at Harvard, I count
ten jets, or maybe forty, one thunder-rivet
no one can sleep through, though many will.
In Prague on the eve of the *Liberation*, you woke
to the Russian troop-planes landing, chain on anvil,
and thought you were back in Cambridge. I wish you were,
up and out on our drag through the two museums,
calling most painters between the Sienese
and the Haitians Greeks. And something else, we've kept
up flirting since the fall of Harry Truman. . . .
Even fools can be crushed by too many girls,

tights, shoes, shirts, underthings, my watch, your bra,
untidy parts that always match. . . . We lay,
something without anything to say.

11 Losers

The tender Falstaffian complaint of Verlaine:
Those who have no minds have more than I;
is it, all drunken words cold sober are true?
Or Valéry's assault on modesty:
To be understood is the worst disaster.
Aside from money, literary success
was small compensation for their vanity:
to be condemned by people who never read them,
to have been useful to poets devoid of talent.
What you should pray for is a thousand readers,
none giving you a hint of his existence,
each thinking your discovery was his secret. . . .
The muse a loser she is sort of sad dirty—
publication might just wash her clean.

12 Sappho

'I set this man above the gods and heroes—
all day he sits before me face to face,
like a cardplayer. My elbow brushes his elbow;
if I should speak, he hears. The touched heart stirs,
the laughter is water hurrying over pebbles. . . .
He is the fairest thing on this dark earth;
I hear him, a hollowness is in my ears,
his footstep. I cannot speak, I cannot see.
A dead whiteness trickles pinpricks of sweat. . . .
I am greener than the greenest green grass;
I can easily make you understand this—

a woman seldom comes to what is best:
her child, her slaves, her daily household ache—
the moon slides west; time gone; I sleep alone.'

13 Good Losers

'Good losers swing this empire by the balls,
we hold all the low cards that take tricks. . . .
I thought we were boozing off our marriages;
mine must have lasted more than thirty years'
nightly immersion in the acid bath. . . .
All marriages are alike. . . . *Sagesse de crise!*
So drunk we snapped our lighters to see the moon;
her room-mate sat reading Simone de Beauvoir till day,
the girl in bed was mouth and two elastics,
three inches of daylight below the blowing shade. . . .
Statesmen have found a girl and moved the state,
they take no step without great pain and harm;
art is happier and breaks a paper dragon. . . .
For the bad loser . . . no word is verbal.'

14 Antony

The righteous rioters once meant revelers,
and had the ear and patronage of kings,
for if the king were Antony, he gave
police protection, and never lost a servant.
If at daybreak he stumbled from heaven to his bed,
next day he bore his winehead like old wine;
yet would notice the fleece of the cirrus, gold, distant,
maidenhair burned in heaven's blue nausée;
then knew he lacked all substance: 'If I could cure
by the Nile's green slot, a page of green papyrus;
I'll taste, God willing, the fruit of the vine no more,

nor Cleopatra, nor the thirsts of sleep.'
'You'd drink the Nile to desert,' she thinks. 'If God
did not exist, this prayer would prove He did.'

15 Aswan Dam

Had Cheops' servants slaved like Nasser's labor,
Russian metal under Russian Foremen,
the pyramid. . . . I saw Russians and imagined
they did more useful work in a day than all Egypt. . . .
Dr. Mohammed Abdullah Fattah al Kassas
tells how the Dam has slowed the downstream drag;
safety dunes and sandbars no longer build
up along the Delta and check the sea,
the Mediterranean drowns a million farms.
Wild water hyacinths evaporate Lake Nasser.
Snails with wormlike bloodflukes slide incurably
to poison five hundred miles of new canals. . . .
Rake-sailed boats once fished the fertile Nile,
Pharaoh's death-ship come back against the tide.

16 For Gallantry

I am ambitious, but the great term ends—
such clouds, rainbows, pink rainstorms, bright green hills,
churches coming and going through the rain,
or wrapped in pale greenish cocoons of mist,
islands, a fleece of quartz, or side of cloud,
on each a friend or two, or dark leaf tree.
I too in the end will see the things like this,
whatever I've lived assumed in one bright glance
like speed-up reading. A lover's back is turned. . . .
This aimless aristocratic anarchy—
where did it take you, do you want to die

like the Earl of Murray, Lover, Stanford White,
Euclides da Cunha shot by husbands?
Did they kill the girl when they killed Achilles?

17 *A Moment*

(PAOLO AND FRANCESCA)

And she to me, 'What sorrow is greater to us
than thinking in misery of the sweet time?
If you will know the first root of our love,
I'll speak as one who must both speak and weep.
On that day we were reading for dalliance
of Lancelot, and how love brought him down;
we were alone there and without suspicion,
often something read made our eyes meet,
and we blushed. A single moment destroyed us: reading
how her loved smile was kissed by such a lover.
This one who never will be divided from me
came shaking to me and kissed my trembling mouth.
That book and he who wrote it was a bawd,
a Galahalt. That day we read no further.'

18 *Wind*

The night blowing on this hospital is human,
Francesca's strife and monotony blown
by the folly of Christendom that loathed her flesh—
seed winds, the youthful breath of the old world,
when each progression of our carnal pleasure
was a firm extension of the soul,
the mammoth mammaries of Aphrodite.
The girl has been rowing her boat since early morning,
her jewelry is twenty wolf teeth pendant.
The snail, a dewdrop, stumbles like the blind,

puts out her little horns to test the sun—
hard riding has never blistered her agile thigh.
This whirlwind, this delirium of Eros—
winds fed the fire, a wind can blow it out.

Abstractions

The virtue of hurry, four or five cars a minute,
lifting the commuter on his great adventure. . . .
But write this feelingly, and out of style—
last 4 A.M. to 7, I lay awake,
my mouth watering for some painless poison;
insomnia flinging everyman to his courage . . .
we live to swell the overpopulation.
Who has done this to me? Drink brought immortal
Faulkner, Crane and Hemingway to himself,
let them plot on inspired when they had died,
less feared by enemies, more feared by friends.
Writer, someone threw the dice out wrong,
or say the chances befriended, not the choices—
or the velocity of conversation.

The Powerful

1 Allah

Like Henry VIII, Mohammed got religion
in the dangerous years, and smashed the celibates,
haters of life, though never takers of lives.
Changed their monasteries to iron-works,
changed their non-activist Buddhistic rote
to his clans' strict laws of *schrecklichkeit* and honor.
The Pope still twangs the harp of chastity;
the boys of the jihad rush paradise
on horseback, roam gardens stocked with adolescent
beauties, both sexes for simple nomad tastes—
ardently they sleep in golden alcoves,
love always renewed, and the air a rose;
woman wants man, man woman, as naturally
as the thirsty frog desires the rain.

2 Attila

Hitler had fingertips of apprehension,
'Who knows how long I'll live? Let us have the war.
We *are* the barbarians, the world is near the end.'
Attila mounted on raw meat and greens
galloped to massacre in his single fieldmouse suit,
he never entered a house that wasn't burning,
could only sleep on horseback, sinking deep
in his rural dream. Would he have found himself
in this coarsest, cruelest, least magnanimous,
most systematic, most philosophical . . .
this sedentary nomad, the 'He who has, has';

who wondered why the ancient world collapsed,
then also left his festering fume of refuse,
old tins, dead vermin, ashes, eggshells, youth?

3 Clytemnestra

No folly can secularize the sacred cow,
our Queen at sixty worked in bed like Balzac.
Once sun and moon lay hidden in the cornstalk,
wherever she moved she left indelible sunset,
she ruled Argos with Pharaoh's beard and beak,
the lower jaw of a waterbuffalo,
the weak intelligence, the iron will.
In one night boys fell ageless from her arms. . . .
Later, something unsavory took place:
Orestes, the lord of murder and proportion,
saw the tips of her nipples had touched her toes—
a population problem and bad art.
He knew the monster must be guillotined.
'I saw her knees to tremble, I enjoyed the sight.'

4 The Death of Count Roland

King Marsiliun in Saragossa
does not love God, he strides to the shade of his orchard,
he sits reclining on his bench of blue tile,
with more than twenty thousand men about him;
his speech is only the one all kings make,
it did to spark the Franco-Moorish War. . . .
At war's-end, Roland's brains seep from his ears;
he calls for the Angel Gabriel, his ivory horn,
prays for his peers, and scythes his sword, Durendal—
farther away than a man might shoot a crossbow,
toward Saragossa, there is a grassy place,

Roland goes to it, climbs the little mound:
a beautiful tree there, four great stones of marble—
on the green grass, he has fallen back, has fainted.

5 The Death of Alexander

The young man's numinous eye is like the sun,
for three days the Macedonian soldiers pass;
speechless, he knows them as if they were his sheep.
Shall the King be carried in the temple
to pray there, and perhaps, recover? But
the god forbids it, saying it is better
Alexander stay where he is. He soon dies,
this after all, perhaps, the 'better' thing. . . .
No one was like him. Terrible were his crimes—
but if you wish to blackguard the Great King,
think how mean, obscure and dull you are,
your labors lowly and your merits less—
this I do know, of all the kings of old,
he alone had the greatness of heart to repent.

6 Tamerlane Old

To wake some midnight, on that instant senile,
clasping clay knees . . . in such warlike posture
found by your grandsons, a sheeted, shivering mound,
pressed race car hideously scared, agog with headlight,
professor in glasses—this is Timur reliving
his pyramid of ninety thousand heads,
not skulls these human heads still fresh as flowers—
an architect to make Vitruvius age.
A thing well done, even a pile of heads
modestly planned to wilt before the builder,
is art, if art is anything won from nature. . . .

We weep for the eyestroke inscrutable not his victims.
The holidays in his journal are mostly massacre—
fealty affirmed when friendship is a myth.

7 Bosworth Field

In a minute, two inches of rain stream through two flat
garden stones, clear as crystal, without trout;
we have gone down and down, gone the wrong brook—
Richard the Third was once Dickon, Duke of Gloucester,
long arm of the realm, goddam blood royal,
terrible underpinning of what could breathe.
No wonder, we have dug him up past proof,
still fighting as if drunk on mortal wounds,
ready to gallop down his own researchers.
Tiberius and Stalin, they killed people they knew.
What does he care for Thomas More and Shakespeare
pointing fingers at his polio'd body;
for the moment, he is king; he is the king
shouting: it's better to have lived, than live.

8 Lady Anne Boleyn

Winter raindrops fling from the roof in crystals;
they wrapped the Lady Anne's head in a white handkerchief....
... To Wolsey, *the nightcrow*; to Victorian dissidents,
Roman virtue spoke from her stubborn lips and chin—
five adulteries in three years of marriage;
the game was too hotly charged. 'I hear say I'll
not die till noon; I am very sorry therefore,
I thought to be dead by this hour and past my pain.'
Her jailer told her beheading was no pain,
'it is so subtle.' 'I have a little neck,'
she said, and put her hands about it laughing.

They guessed she had much pleasure and joy in death—
no foreigners admitted, but thanks to her Husband,
the scene was public to all nativeborn Englishmen.

9 Charles V by Titian

But we cannot go back to Charles V
barreled in armor, more gold fleece than king;
he haws on the gristle of a Flemish word,
his upper and lower Hapsburg jaws won't meet.
The sunset he tilts at is big Venetian stuff,
the true Charles, done by Titian, never lived.
The struggle he rides offstage to is offstage.
No St. Francis, he did what Francis shied at,
gave up office, one of twenty monarchs
since Saturn to willingly make the grand refusal.
In his burgherish monastery, he learned he couldn't
even put together the wheels of a clock.
He had dreamed of the democracy of Europe,
and carried enemies with him in a cage.

10 The Army of the Duc de Nemours

'I am a Christian because I am a wanton';
not Yeats this, who warned us not to lend a high
degree of reality to the Great War.
There are wars and wars, though ours are not the high-note
on the scale of sexual delirium
running the gamut of Moses' anathemas:
wantonness, sodomy, bestiality.
The Italian mercenaries besieging Lyons
for the Duc de Nemours huzzaed great flocks
of goats before them—no billies, two thousand udders
decked up in sporty green coats trimmed with gold.

They served a sound man as a mistress. Small war,
one far distant from our army mascots;
and who remembers now what Lyons paid?

11 Marlowe

Vain surety of man's mind so near to death,
twenty-nine years and free to total fifty—
one blurred, hurried, still undecoded month
hurled Marlowe from England to his companion shades;
his dead words rise from the rest of night to reason. . . .
How uncontrollably sweet and swift his life,
with two fresh hits and riding his high season,
drinking May out at Deptford with three friends,
one or all four perhaps in Secret Service.
Christ was a bastard, His Testament's filthily greeked—
he died swearing, stabbed among friends who loved him
discussing the barcheck. . . . Tragedy means to die . . .
for that vacant parsonage, Posterity,
tabloid stamped in bronze, our deeds in dust.

12 Mary Stuart

They ran for their lives up nightslope, gained the car,
the girl's maxi-coat, Tsar officer's, dragged the snow,
she and he killed her husband, they stained the snow.
Romance of the snowflakes! Men swam up the night,
grass pike in overalls with scythe and pitchfork;
shouting, 'Take the car, we'll smash the girl.'
Once kings were on firstname terms with the poor,
a car was a castle, and money belonged to the rich. . . .
They roared off hell-wheel and scattered the weak mob;
happily only one man splashed the windshield,
they dared not pluck him, it was hard at night

to hold to the road with a carcass on the windshield—
at nightmare's end, the bedroom, dark night of marriage,
the bloodiest hands were joined and took no blood.

13 Bishop Berkeley

The Bishop's nihilism is clerical,
no one was much imperiled by his life,
except he visited Newport and was Irish,
he was not Rimbaud or Attila,
unhinged, pleased to crack the world on his skull.
He lived with quality, and thought the world
is only the perceptions we perceive. . . .
In Mexico, I met this private earthquake,
when the soil trembled in the soles of my feet;
it was only my high blood of the decline,
my river system saying: I am weak,
I am Whitman, I am Berkeley . . . all men,
bathing my feet in a tub of lukewarm water;
one foot scalds the water, one foot chills the water.

14 Robespierre and Mozart as Stage

Robespierre could live saying, 'The republic
of Virtue without *la terreur* is disaster,'
saying, 'Loot the chateaux, spare Saint Antoine,'
saying to Danton, 'I'll love you till I die,'
Clean prisons! They learned the guillotine is painless—
La Revolution, her old Jacobin saying:
'The theater must remain and remain theater,
play for the traditional, barren audience orgy,
play back the Revolution. . . .' Ask the true voyeur
what blue movie is worth a seat at the keyhole. . . .
Even the prompted Louis Seize was living theater,

sternly but lovingly judged by critics, who knew
a Mozart's insolent slash at folk could never
cut the gold thread of the suffocating curtain.

15 Saint-Just: 1767-1793

Saint-Just: the name seems stolen from the Missal. . . .
He thought only the laconic fit to rule.
His chamois coat, the dandy's vast cravat
knotted with pretentious negligence;
he carried his head like the Holy Sacrament.
If such a man wants to enlighten the world,
he must move with the stone footstep of the sun—
faction follows the course of revolution,
as reptiles follow the course of a torrent.
'I'm twenty, I've done badly, I'll do better;'
he did, he reached the scaffold, *'Je sais où je vais.*
I am young and therefore close to nature.
Happiness is a new idea in Europe;
we've bronzed liberty with the guillotine.'

16 Coleridge and King Richard

Coleridge wasn't flatter-blinded by
his ties with Richard II . . . a *feminine friendism,*
a constant overflow of imagination
proportioned to a dwindling will to act.
Richard unkinged saw shipwreck in the mirror,
his face was not the King's; womanlike, he saw
he must look at himself frequently to exist. . . .
White glittering inertia of the iceberg—
it was a comforting fancy that only blacks
could cherish enslavement for two hundred years;
most negroes in London had onwardlooking thoughts

by 1800, moved farther from the jungle
and reveries of kings, than Coleridge,
the poet who blamed his failure on himself.

17 Northwest Savage

With people like the great silent majority,
the great people can't get elected President;
but Chicago, Detroit, Lincoln owe their rise
to Harrison, selfish little busybody
expelling Indians, legalizing negroes,
losing most of his battles with the Savage,
if numbers were anything equal. No acid worked more
mechanically on vegetable fibre
than the whites in number. . . . Did the fish fighting
have leisure to see the waters had collapsed,
that even Jefferson's philanthropy
offered the great award for their extinction?
For landthirst, whiskeythirst? I flip extinct matches
at your rhinocerous hide . . . inflammable earth.

18 Old Hickory

Those awful figures of Yankee prehistory;
the prints were cheap once, and good faith came easy:
Stephen Decatur, spyglass screwed to raking
the cannonspout-smashed Bay of Tripoli—
still, the Mohammedan believes in war;
although we had no faith to send their souls
to heaven, we were death on piracy.
Some were democratic: primitive, high-toned
President Jackson on his hobby horse,
watermelon-slice hat and presentation sword;
he might have been the Tsar or Bolivar,

pillar of the right or pillar of the left—
Andrew Jackson, despite appearances,
stands for the gunnery that widened suffrage.

19 Abraham Lincoln

All day I bang and bang at you in thought,
as if I had the licence of your wife,
miles past the border of intimate disrespect. . . .
Your War, a continuation of politics—
that's the word for a Lincoln or Bismark . . . or,
politics is the continuation of murder.
You, our one genius in politics . . . you followed
the bull to the altar, death in unity.
J'accuse, j'accuse, j'accuse, j'accuse, j'accuse!
Say it in American. Who'll shoot the deserters?
Winter blows sparks in the face of the new God,
who breathes in fire and dies of cooling faith,
as the firebrand turns black in the black hand,
and the squealing pig darts sidewise from his foot.

20 Sunrise

There's always enough sunrise in hell to gasp the breeze;
the flower of what was left grew sweeter for them,
two done people conversing with bamboo fans
as if brushing the firefall from their yard—
Admiral Onishi is still a cult to his juniors
for launching the Kamikazes; he became an osprey
by mistaking our armadas for game;
his pilots loved him to annihilation.
He chats in his garden, the sky is zigzags of fire.
One butchery is left; his wife keeps nagging.
Man and wife taste cup after cup of Scotch;

how garrulously they talk about their grandchildren,
and when the knife goes home, it goes home wrong. . . .
For eighteen hours you died with your hand in hers.

21 F. O. Matthiessen: 1902-1950

Matthiessen jumping from the North Station hotel,
breaking his mania barrier to despair;
a prophet to the dead Czech-student torches?
Or manslaughter? Who knows whom he might have killed,
falling bald there like a shell. I'm scared
to hit this street, or stand like Stonewall Jackson
spitting on the superhighways. I wouldn't
be murdered, or even murder, for my soul;
no one has a good face to die in war—
Mattie, his Yale *Skull and Bones* on the dresser, torn
between the homosexual's terrible love
for forms, and his anarchic love of man . . .
then dies, unique as the many, lies frozen meat,
fast colors lost to lust and prosecution.

22 New Year's Eve 1968

These conquered kings pass angrily away;
the gods die flesh and spirit and last in print,
each library is some injured tyrant's home.
This year runs out in the movies, it must be written
in bad, straightforward, unscanning sentences—
mine were downtrodden, branded on backs of carbons,
lines, words, letters nailed to letters, words, lines;
the typescript looked like a Rosetta Stone.
A year's black pages. Its hero *hero demens*
forcing his ship past soundings to the passage—
ill-starred of men and crossed by his fixed stars.

The slush-ice on the east water of the Hudson
is rose-heather this New Year sunset; the open channel,
bright sky, bright sky, carbon scarred with ciphers.

1970 New Year

By miracle, I left the party half
an hour behind you, reached home five hours drunker. . . .
To live a million years, and a million years
longer than the gods on Olympus or Jutland
would be too short to polish up this tarnish.
The gods, employed to haunt and punish husbands,
have no eye for trigger-fine distinctions;
their myopia makes all error mortal.
My Darling, prickly hedgehog of the hearth,
chocolates, cherries, hairshirt, pinks and glass—
when we drank in the first blindness of courtship,
loving lost half its vice with all its virtue.
Who wants a second life and two more wives?
Cards will never be dealt us fairly again.

April's End

1 King David Senex

Two or three times a night, and for a month,
we wrang the night-sweat from his shirt and sheets;
on the fortieth day, we brought him Abishag,
and he recovered, and he knew her not—
cool through the hottest summer day, and moist;
her rankness more delicate than all the flowers,
as if her urine caused the vegetation,
Jerusalem leaping from the golden dew;
but later, the Monarch's well-beloved shaft
lay quaking in place; they thought the world was flat,
yet half the world was hanging on each breast,
as two spent swimmers that did cling together;
Sion come to Israel, if they had held. . . .
This clinch is quickly broken, they were glad to break.

2 Night-Sweat

Work-table, litter, books and standing lamp,
plain things, my stalled equipment, the old broom—
but I am living in a tidied room,
for ten nights now I've felt the creeping damp
float over my pajamas' wilted white. . . .
Sweet salt embalms me and my head is wet,
everything streams and tells me this is right;
my life's fever is soaking in night-sweat—
one life, one writing! But the downward glide
and bias of existing wrings us dry—
always inside me is the child who died,

always inside me is his will to die—
one universe, one body . . . in this urn
the animal night-sweats of the spirit burn.

3 Caligula

My namesake, Little Boots, Caligula,
you disappoint me. Tell me what you saw—
Item: your body hairy, badly made,
head hairless, smoother than your marble head;
Item: eyes hollow, hollow temples, red
cheeks roughed with rouge, legs spindly, hands that leave
a clammy snail's trail on your wilting sleeve,
your hand no hand can hold . . . bald head, thin neck—
you wished the Romans had a single neck.
That was no artist's bubble. Animals
ripened for your arenas suffered less
than you when slaughtered—yours the lawlessness
of something simple that has lost its law,
my namesake, not the last Caligula.

4 Goiter Tests: Werner von Usslingen

Half eggshell, half eggshell, and white the glass of water;
the whiteness soaked and doubled by the water,
soft goiter croaking for a plaster-cast,
heads flayed to the bone like Leonardo's felons,
deaf heads thrust forward at me not to hear,
lipping with the astuteness of the deaf.
Eggshells that rub like boughs. This double thing
more bone than any skull, it isn't me—
this I, this moment I, will die and leave
my thumbprint immovable on my plaster-cast. . . .
Many times fear, fame, fatuity will bring

self to the self, to Werner von Usslingen,
his pure shield carved with German landsknecht French:
L'ennemi de Dieu et de merci.

5 Rush

God help the headlong rush of this existence,
the sobs of Zeus and Hera who knew any
woman must love her husband more than her,
constantly hated and inconstantly loved.
Men married, then made a mangod; he was single:
some Mongol who took refreshment from a flower,
the fading petals the color of fresh wood—
'I was made by a girl in the summer heat.'
My friend finds hope in China, 'The plan's a small thing,
as if I were drowning and flying at the same time.
I am no spy just a mediocre student.'
Hope is the must-be, the tomb of a small child:
Say, Passerby, that man is born to die—
Iknaton with spikes of the gold sun in his hair.

6 Nostalgie de la Boue

The lines string out from nowhere, stretch to sorrow.
I think of others who were prominent,
the ironclads in any literary havoc,
now even lost to malice. 'He exists,'
as the old Stalinist luminary said of a friend
sent to Siberia, 'Cold helps him to compose.'
Sometimes for days I only hear one voice,
one shirt may last a winter and a day.
As a child my other wife climbed a chair to dress;
'It was easier.' It's easier to miss food,
not brush my teeth, flinch off new mail;

the Muse shouts vacation in my ear:
nostalgie de la boue that shelters ape
and protozoa from the rights of man.

Eloges to the Spirits

1 Revenants

They come back sometimes, we know they do,
freed like felons on the opening days of May;
if there's a healthy bite in the south wind,
Spring the echo of heaven's single day,
they sun naked like earthworms on the puddly mall.
They are better equipped for everything than people,
except perhaps for living. If we met them
covertly enough, I think we could name them all:
Cousin So, Ancestral Mother-in-Law So . . .
but we cannot laugh them into smiling back;
'A shade,' they say, 'is more readily killed than blackmailed.'
With misty bounds they scale the starry sheer,
stare blood-eyed down into our poignant dog-yap—
as little wanting our dust as we want theirs.

2 Verdun

I bow down to the great goiter of Verdun,
and know what's waiting, ivory telephone,
ribs, hips, pale machinegun bleached to parchment;
they lie fatigued from too much punishment,
hang by a string to friends they knew first-hand,
to the God of our fathers still twenty like themselves.
Their medals and rosettes keep in bloom,
they stay young, only living makes us age.
I see the town they came from, twelve streets of brownstone,
cleft by a rectilinear central garden,
a formal gesture and a slice of life.

The city says, 'I am the finest city. . . .
This landmass held by half a million bodies
for Berlin or Paris, twin cities saved at Verdun.

3 Hydrotherapy

No beer or washrag, half the lightbulbs busts,
still the dump was free and a gift for a king—
its rows of tubs like church-pews, infinite,
on each a reading-board, a pair of glasses,
a cake of scouring soap and Proust in French—
men and women indistinguishable,
each breast, as the sons of Belial dreamed, a chest;
our groins were pure and fit to bear a church.
We are like our backs. We, who have been wet and cold,
soak, and for the first time in our lives are dry.
But Adam's gums still leave blood on the apple;
we can't be all things, eat the spit of the snake,
then gaze with the naked candor of the Tsar,
his slightly bald Medusa's pewter eye.

4 Words for a Guinea-Pig

'Of late they leave the light on by my entry,
so I won't scare, though I never scare in the dark;
I bless this arrow that flies from wall to window—
five years and a nightlight given me to breathe;
Heidegger said that time is ecstasy. . . .
I was not scared, although my life was short,
my sickly breathing the friendly chaff of leather.
Mrs. Muffin! It clicks. I had my day.
They will paint me like Cromwell with all my warts:
small mop with a tumor and eyes too popped for thought;
I was like a rhinoceros when jumped by my sons.

I ate and bred, and then I only ate,
my life that reached its zenith in the 'sixties—
this short pound God threw on the scales, found wanting.

A Second Plunge, A Dream

What I have written was arranged to happen:
to waken on the window's measured ledge,
it soon apparent that I will not cling
hugging my shins, and whistle daylight home
through the chalk and catlight of the ancient city,
Rome of Caesar's division and sunstick palms.
I've lived to the vibration of fulfilment;
the bash is a light sentence for my plunge
past galleried windows of the neighbor house,
this shadow built between the sun and me
gagging on the eaten air in the wellshaft.
The only sun I get is off these windows,
3–3.30: direct reflected sun
man in prison—Gramsci in Rome reflecting
optimism of will, pessimism of intelligence.

For Norman Mailer

The 9 A.M. man on the street is new
and still the many, and he moves; he moves
in one direction for Fifth Avenue,
and up Fifth Avenue, simplex as the pigeons,
as crocked with project, and his heart, a watch,
imagines being paid for being on time. . . .
Straight Buenos Aires, . . . everyman walks the clock,
his heart on Greenwich, the West's last Anglophile,
his constitutionals a reek of tweed;
in B.A. the girls have never missed their dates. . . .
Siren of noon, I wait here. Norman Mailer,
his wardrobe two identical straight blue suits
and two blue vests to prove monotony,
disproves the many false faces I see as one.

May

1 The Pacification of Columbia

Patches of tan and blood-warm rooftile, azure:
an old jigsawpuzzle Mosque of Omar flung
to vaultless consummation and blue consumption,
exhalation of the desert sand to fire.
I got the message, one the puzzle never sent. . . .
No destructive element emaciates
Columbia this Mayday afternoon;
the thickened buildings look like buildings out
of Raphael, colossal classic, dungeon feudal;
horses, higher artistic types than their grooms,
forage Broadway's median trees, as if
nature were liberated . . . the blue police
lean on the burnished, nervous hides, show they,
at least, have learned to meet and reason together.

May 1, 1968

2 Can a Plucked Bird Live?

From the first cave, the first farm, the first sage,
inalienable our human right to murder—
'You must get used,' they say, 'to the thought of guns;
you must get used to seeing guns; you must
get used to using guns.' Guns too are mortal. Guns
failed Che Guevara, Marie Antionette,
Leon Trotsky, the children of the Tsar:
chivalrous ornaments to power. Tom Paine said
Burke pitied the plumage and forgot the dying bird;
tight times can use the caustic pamphleteer—

arms in the hands of the people are criminal,
arms given the people are always used against the people;
the only guns that will not kill the owner
are forged by raised hands . . . fear made wise by anger.

3 Leader of the Left

Love will not bind it to his blind ambition,
or blinder courage (both sowed their dirty germs)
or some ostracizing glandular unbalance;
it was his miracle that closed his eyes,
when his whole face took on a flesh of wood,
slab of raw plastic grafted to his one
natural feature, scars from the demonstrations,
he bore like a Heidelberg student for the New Left.
His voice, electric, was a low current whir;
by now he'd bypassed sense and even eloquence;
without listening, the audience understood;
anticipating the sentence, they too stood
for the predestined poignance of his murder,
his Machiavellian Utopia of pure nerve.

4 The Restoration

The old king enters his study with the police;
it's much like mine left in my hands a month:
unopened letters, the thousand cigarettes,
open books, yogurt cups in the unmade bed—
the old king enters his study with the police,
but all in all, his study is much worse than mine;
an edge of malice puts the seal of man:
frames smashed, their honorary honors lost,
all the unopened letters have been answered.

He halts at woman-things that can't be his,
he says, 'To think that human beings did this!'
The sergeant picks up a defiled *White Goddess*, or is it
Secret Memoirs of the Courts of Europe?
'Would a human beings do this things to these book?'

5 Chienlit

Seldom fine virtue without true words; yet he
who dumbly guns his government on virtue
is like the northern star, which keeps its place,
which keeps its place, and all the stars turn to it;
asks faithfulness and sincerity, though these
do more for usurpers than the tyranny;
while he, unseeing, says: a true man acts,
then speaks, speaks in accordance with his act:
what is good for the swarm is good for the bee—
learning without thought is labor lost;
and thought without learning? It is perilous;
as if law could be the fulfilment of love,
leaving freedom to be invisible,
piss in any direction on your lawn.

6 The Ark

Time lost, when we enjoyed perverse harangues,
and hit the scientists with Plato's corkscrew—
youth! I wanted an art as disciplined
and dark as Calvin in his *Institutes*,
our stop was meter; Shakespeare wrote the last play—
but now there're no takers for this argument. . . .
Two buildings, two futures, go up across the street;
one at Harvard, the other in New York;
one churns at six, the other at six-thirty,

but best the men shouting on the wooden ribs—
thus on the ribs of the Ark and in his cups,
Noah harangued the world he wished to save. . . .
How could the reckless, authoritative young
bear us, if we were given length of days?

7 The New York Intellectual

How often was this last salute recast?
Did Irving really want three hundred words,
such tact and tough, ascetic resonance,
the preposition *for*, five times in parallel,
to find himself 'a beleaguered minority,
without fantasies of martyrdom,'
facing the graves of the New York Intellectuals,
'without joy, but neither with dismay'?
This art was needed for his final sentence;
others see the entombment with dismay.
How often one would choose the poorman's provincial
out of town West Side intellectual
for the great brazen rhetorician serpent,
swimming the current with his iron smile!

8 In the American Grain

'Eleven, and bicycling into the stone sun,
I was in love. I was half-wasp already,
and changed my shirt and trousers twice a day. . . .
My books returned. I live in a Jewish state,
swaying its insomniac minorities.
I am weary of enlightenment:
what Wall Street prints, the mafia distributes;
when talent starves in a garret, they buy the garret.
Williams made less than neckties on his writing,

he could never learn the King's English of *The New Yorker.*
Sooner or later, everything good gets printed;
time even stoops to merit. Dr. Williams
saw the germ on every flower, and knew
the snake is a petty, rather pathetic creature.'

9 Dropout

'Sailboats are still out, though the saltmarsh is hay;
back for the funeral in the old town, New London,
I see the names of men instead of men.
What did I do to myself? I painted, mostly
using my hand for a brush. I might be someone,
if I could be photographed twenty-four hours a day.
My peer-group, student, ex-student, no-student, mean less
to me than Irish dropouts of sixty in bars. . . .
But Father believed the country needed strong men
like Harry Truman—Father was a bang
to do Japan with: he was never stoned,
never irrelevant; at each airport,
he did five postcards, or recorded history—
my background had no talent for using sloth.'

10 The Dissenting Academy

The Moslem's hack-moon hangs over WABC
TELEVISION, with its queue of stand-ins;
real trees, the sky-distempered, skim of winter,
tremble on the yellow, nondescript brick tower—
our city! No garden city curbs more poodles,
our iron grinds like a hundred kinds of birds;
that's us, it isn't worth writing home about,
this is our home. . . . The scholar escapes his time;
college depression darkens his small-pane window,

ivy gross as grapeleaf. His students prime the pump,
till he wattles like a turkey to his grant.
Scholarship proves the scholar less than mortal;
why should anyone settle for New York?
Dying without death is a life in the city.

11 *The Doctor*

(ELOISE AND ABELARD)

We know what orthodox analysis
could do with her, the talented, the taloned
cat hooked on the cold fish of Abelard.
They had one mind once, now his brain is bone,
and her neglected ember is extinct.
After his prison, to the woman came
energy such as she never knew before,
sprinkling on us like a fresh flow of blood,
old Sorbonne argot, filth for Saint Bernard,
untimely, mystical, sold to the police. . . .
Abelard's tortured debater's points
fly to the mark, feathered with her ecstasy—
his student crushes, and his fall like lightning,
in love with the dialectic, his Minerva. . . .

12 *West Side Sabbath*

(*Breakfast*)

WIFE, in her tower of *The New York Sunday Times*;
HUSBAND, rewriting his engagement-book. . . .
WIFE: Nixon's in trouble. HUSBAND: Another family
brawl? WIFE: Nixon's got profounder trouble.
HUSBAND: You mean our National Peace Offensive?
WIFE: *Entre autres.* HUSBAND: When Nixon weighs in,
does he outweigh *The New York Sunday Times*?

189

WIFE: Say that twice, and I'll drown myself with Bruce. . . .
Are we *the* Left, a monochrome Socialism,
Robespierre's gunpoint equality,
privilege slashed to a margin of survival?
Or student-Left, a casually defined
anarchists' faith in playing the full deck—
who wants the monks without the fucking Maypole?

13 Revenant

(FOR MARY MCCARTHY)

'*The land going down to the lake was choked with wild rose,*
the fruit was stuck to golden, the high swans, drunk
on making love, had plunged their aching heads;
the water was rebirth, but then the winter:
no flower, or sun, or most times field for shadow—
exhaust and airconditioning klir in the wind. . . .
The real motive for my trip is dentistry,
a descending scale: long ago, I used to drive
to New York to see a lover, next the analyst,
then an editor, then a lawyer, last . . .
I can't quite make this the Seven Ages of Man.
Faith is in labor; I fear I am one of the few
sane people living . . . a not too stunning sensation—
they want something different from understanding: belief.'

14 New York

We must have had a lift once from New York
thirty years back, or two; it's hard to think,
gone like Sunday mahjong and netting butterflies—
someone comes here from the outlands, Trinidad,
tuned to another metropolis, Port of Spain;
deplanes here, knowing no one, strapped, thirsty
to hoof the street of wonder. . . . Each plateglass

display looks a nightclub from a block away,
each nightclub Islam with its liveried tariff,
all the money, all the connection. . . . One has none,
triggered for the liberated girl with a build,
seeker bayonetted at the barricade—
Frederick the Great of Prussia's war-cheer, 'Move,
you bastards, do you want to live forever?'

15 Open House

'*You hitting a girl, you're hitting the Virgin Mary.*'
—His face is a Vesuvius of his vomit.
—You'd erupt yourself if you carried his dead weight.
—Whites never forgive you if you use them drunk.
—This boy's rugged, he's holding the toilet bowl.
—He's licking the shower-curtain, he's that thirsty.
Black plastic curtain makes a man a raincoat,
ask Whitey. Only one Whitey, he's the landlady.
—He's trying to part his hair on the phone-receiver.
—Wants a soul-dimension for his brain.
—Now he's phoning his cat in Gary, Indiana.
It's too far from Boston to stick his tongue—No, listen,
he's talking, listen: '*You believe in love,
some use for poverty outside imagination. . . .*'

16 Sounds in the Night

Nothing new in them yet their old rôles startle;
asked to adapt, they swear they cannot swerve:
machines are the only servants bound to serve us,
metal, mortal and mechanical,
their dissonance varied as our northern birds—
clear and singing through the night air dirt!
Sleepless I drink their love, if it is love.

Miles below heaven, luminous in some courtyard,
dungeoned by primitive wall-brick windowless,
the grass conservative cry of the cat in heat—
'Who cares if the running stream is sometimes stopped?
Inexhaustible the springs from which I flow.'
Cats will be here when man is prehistory,
man doomed to outlast his eternal work.

17 Civilization

Your skirt stopped half a foot above my knee,
personal birthmarks varied your black mesh,
and yet I praise your legs as generic legs—
and who would want to finger or approach
what ruminated through your printed sweater?
Civilization will always outdo life,
its toleration means to bear and ache,
hate, hurt oneself, as no one wants to twice.
That's Locke, that's Mill; the Liberal lies with that,
bites his own lip to show his icy tooth.
That's why there are none, that's why we are none,
why the worst bastard shivers once a moon,
if the god Eros arcs into the Virgin;
as you, no virgin, made me bear myself.

18 Publication Day

'Dear Robert: I wish you were not a complete stranger,
I wish I knew something more about your mercy,
could total your minimum capacity
for empathy—this varies so much from genius.
Can you fellow-suffer for a turned-down book?
Can you see past your tragic vision, and
have patience with one isolated heart?

Do you only suffer for other famous people,
and socially comforting non-entities?
Has the thistle of failure a place in your affection?
It's important to know these things; in your equestrian
portrait by Mailer, I don't find these things. . . .
I write as a woman flung from a sinking ship—
one raft in the distance . . . you represent that raft.'

19 *The Hunt*

For months the drowth of love has kept me marching,
now I am healthy, and I cannot stand;
women see through me like a head of cheese—
see enamelled on the gold goiter band
men from the costume shop of Botticelli,
men in ultra-violet tights and doublets,
coiffures of Absalom; they probe my thicket
with pikes and swingnets, and I try to breathe,
I try to keep up breathing while I hide.
These are not Tuscan or Roman mercenaries;
this is England, main artery of fighting—mercy was murder
at Towton when King Edward's heralds counted
twenty thousand Lancastrian dead in the field,
doubling the number as they made the count.

20 *The Diamond Cutters*

That terrible late October summer day;
we passed the diamond cutters and appraisers,
hole-in-the-corners on 47th Street—
trade ancient as the Ur-kings' bank-account,
loss of empire for a grain of dust;
all was in essence, rare and hard and bright.
Herman Melville would have had the meaning,

while gritting his final dogdays in New York,
far from his cousin dogfish and white whale;
but no one can avoid the thoughts of man:
mason's chisel on the throat of a stone. . . .
We were boulevarding out the time till lunch;
the conversation was inaudible to You,
eye brighter than the uncut sun at noon.

21 The Picture

(FOR ELIZABETH)

This might be nature—twenty stories high,
two water tanks, tobacco shingle, girdled
by stapled pasture wire, while bed to bed,
we lie gazing into the ether's crystal ball,
sky and a sky and sky and sky, till death . . .
my heart stops, this might be heaven. Twenty years
ago, we shot for less, could settle for
a picture, out of style then and now in,
of seven daffodils. We watched them blow:
buttercup yellow were the flowers, and green
the stems as fresh paint, over them the wind,
the blowzy wooden branches of the elms,
the sack of hornets sopping up the flame—
still over us, still in parenthesis.

22 Lunch Date

Mullioned windows of a Madison Avenue British pub,
one's astream with noonday, the other sundown,
stream on the grander glass of a sporting print:
Old England tarted up with boor and barmaid,
her color roused and rouged by horsier custom,
as a reflection elevates the coarse.

Often color lines are dulled and blurred
in the great city, and exotics mate.
I touch your lifeline; no one is disarmed,
or handcuffed. It's not malevolence but inertia
gives men the legs to meet their obligations.
Is it active sloth that ties our hands?
Two windows, two reflections, one bypasser
doubled and hurrying from the double life.

23 Piano Practice

(FOR ADRIENNE RICH)

Trained at four to read a score by Mozart,
perched on *Plutarch's Lives* to reach the keyboard,
paid a raisin for each note struck true—
in your piano pastel, you keep practice,
your style attuned and stylized by the painter. . . .
Then round, round haired, married, a mother, comes
the season of your rash fling at playing bourgeois. . . .
Now thin, one loose lock tossed . . . the splendid must fall,
'*Montaigne, you bastard!*' We've robbed the arsenal
to feed the needy, Toussaint, Fanon, Malcolm,
the Revolution's *mutilés de guerre*,
shirtless ones dying, killing on the rooftops—we too,
disabled veterans, how long will we bay with the hounds
and beat time with crutches? Your groundnote was joy.

24 Memorial Day

Sometimes I sink a thousand centuries,
bone tired or stone asleep, to sleep ten seconds—
voices, their future voices, adolescents,
go crowding through the chilling open windows:
fathomless profundities of inanimation.

And we will be, then, and as they are here.
But nothing will be put back right in time,
done over, thought through straight again—not my father
revitalizing in a simple Rhineland spa,
Mussolini's misguiding roosterstep
in the war year, just before *our* War began. . . .
Ah, ah, this house of twenty-foot apartments,
all the windows yawning—the voices of its tutees,
their fortissimo *Figaro*, sunk into dead brick.

Robert Kennedy 1925-1968

1 R.F.K.

Hire in my workroom, in its listlessness
of Vacancy, some old Victorian house,
airtight and sheeted for old summers,
far from the hornet yatter of the bond—
is loneliness, a thin smoke thread of vital
air. What can I catch from you now?
Doom was woven in your nerves, your shirt,
woven in the great clan; they too were loyal,
and you too were loyal to them, to death.
For them like a prince, you daily left your tower
to walk through dirt in your best cloth. Untouched,
alone in my Plutarchan bubble, I miss
you, you out of Plutarch, made by hand—
forever approaching our maturity.

2 Another Circle

The modulation is most alive and firm,
when three or four colors are about the same,
when three or four words sound much the same,
clear without monopoly—not us,
this first ride of summer, Harriet: I trapped in words,
you gagging your head-over-heels articulation.
The search. The circle. We can't hunt God. He hunts us,
and his story is sad . . . the Irish in black, three rows
ranked for the future photograph, the Holy Name,
fiercely believed in then, then later held to
perhaps more fiercely in their unbelief.

How they hated to leave this unpremeditated
gesture of their life! No Name can judge their killer,
his guiltless liver, kidneys, fingertips and phallus.

3 Another June

Nervous leaves twitter on the high wood tree,
this and that thing, grape-purple, skims the lawn,
night shrouds the monopolies of Rome and Carthage,
the oil is spent, the oilpumps seesaw thirst.
Who can believe the nesting, sexing tree swallow
would dive for an eye or brain . . . this handbreadth insect,
navy butterfly, the harbinger of rain,
change to danger in this twilight? Will we
swat out the birds as ruthlessly as flies? . . .
One was refreshed when you wisecracked through the guests,
usually somewhat woodenly, hoarsely dry,
pure Celt on the eastern seaboard. Who was worse stranded?
Is night only your torchlight wards gone black,
white wake on wave, pyre set for the fire that fell?

To Summer

1 The Worst Sinner

The earliest sportsman in our earliest dawn,
waking to what redness, waking a killer,
saw the red cane was sweet in his red grip;
the blood of the sheep matched the blood of the wolf;
yet Jonathan Edwards learned how to think himself
worse than any man that ever breathed;
he was a good man, and he thought with reason—
which of us hasn't thought the same thought worse?
Each night I lie me down to sleep in rest;
two or three times a week, I wake to my sin—
sins, not sin; not two or three days, seven.
God himself cannot wake up five years younger,
and drink away the chalice of our death-sentence,
like the best man in the best possible world.

2 God of Our Fathers

Say it's the one-way trip, the one-way flight,
strip the worse meaning from *trip* and *flight*;
then you could say you stood in the cold light of science,
seeing as you are seen, espoused to fact.
Strange, a life is the fire and fuel; we,
the animals, the objects, must be here
without a title-deed of evidence
that anything that ever stopped living
ever falls back to living when life stops.
There's more romance to the watchmaker God
of Descartes and Paley; He drafted and installed

the Apparatus for us. He loved to tinker—
Who having perfected what He had to do,
stood off shrouded in his loneliness.

3 *White*

This summer night, and then *the* summer night,
windows reflecting lighted on that white—
the door between is not the door between:
the Sabines, Casanova's weeping willow,
Death dropping his white marble scythe, our brother,
one skeleton among the skeletons. . . .
Ghengis and Attila killed fewer of their kind.
This kind is only expelled by prayer and fasting;
yet we were no kinder when we had the Faith,
and thought the massacred could be reformed,
and move like angels in the unwithering white,
file upon file, the beds of long-neck clams,
blue-white and hard and sharp and stiff and pure—
the clam-shell cunted in the ground of being.

4 *Heaven*

Smoke weakens the dim greens of Mexico,
the City, not the nation; as if field fires
of marijuana fumed in the back yards.
One breathes the green dust as the end of life,
as though it were heaven. Some child or cubist flays
the gardens of Versailles to cube, cone and ball—
this shouldn't strain our imagination—heaven
if we can be there, must be perfect. I've been there,
seen the Sun-King spit into the wind of Versailles;
he cannot tell his left hand from his right,
he holds up two smooth stones, marked *left* and *right*. . . .

In the straight hall, the straighter curtains lift,
a head higher, two heads higher, than the old shrunk King;
they dance spontaneously in the atheist air.

5 Quality I

(FOR JOAN DICK)

'I opened, shed bright musk. . . . For eighty years?
The high heel squeaks, the square shoe fits the foot—
it's not a girl's, her charm against the dragons,
walking the night in circles to flee the fire. . . .
In my sleep last night, we were in the flames of a barge,
the angry water out of calling below;
I had to choose jumping or scrambling down
the sighing hull. I clasped your hands. I woke so. . . .
One can be washed white in the foam of the divine.
This once? No, almost at will when one is young;
this ends since God is quality,
one I could never do without or with:
ears that heard not, mouth that said not, eyes. . . .
The tree God looked at speaks to the other trees.'

6 Quality II

'Life never comes with both hands full.
One is told there is nothing one can do
to help others. Well, I don't mind that—
in the past I spent too much time travelling
from sister to sister each time they felt *down*.
Now it's as though we played a game of Still Pond:
no more moves. I ask, status quo
satisfaction for all no-downs, please God,
and not too many ups for others. That's why
the Virgin Mary means so much to down-men,
to all people so far out they can't take calls,

old hearts, no man's pleasure, gone to the eye of envy . . .
though I am in tears, I am appeased.'

7 The House-Party

(FOR LOUIS MACNEICE, 1907–1963)

Two dozen children would visit half a dozen;
downstairs the lost child bullied the piano,
getting from note to note like jumping railties;
the black keys showed their bruises and turned white.
The games he heard outside and missed were no
less crudely commonplace and solidly hit—
no need to be Bach to be what we are. . . .
Once you watched your father, the Bishop, wade
up-trout-stream barefoot, you liked him, 'What poor feet! . . .
Until I was almost thirty, I thought
some woman might roll on me, and smother me.'
A month from his death, we stood by Epstein's bust
of Bertrand Russell; Louis said, 'It's better
to die at fifty than lose my pleasure in terror.'

8 For Theodore Roethke 1908–1963

At Yaddo, you shared a bathroom with a bag
tree-painter whose boobs bounced in the basin,
your blues basin where you wished to plunge your head. . . .
All night, my friend, no friend, you swam my sleep;
this morning you are lost in the Maine sky,
close, cold and gray, smoke, smoke-colored cloud.
Sheeplike, unsociable, reptilian, the shags
fling in straight lines like duck in a shooting booth,
divers devolving to a monochrome.
You honored nature, helpless, elemental
creature, and touched the waters of the offing;

you left them quickened with your name: Ted Roethke. . . .
Omnipresent, the Mother made you nonexistent,
you, the ocean's anchor, our high tide.

9 Professors of Tenure

They'd murder for a chair, ask alms for sitting;
these too were students, knelt to the green elder,
the voice in these alders: *Of course they have the bomb;*
what's wanting is the nerve to play the music,
smash East Germany and Poland in two days,
burn Russia with our nuclear typhoon,
blast Cairo, Damascus, Baghdad back to sand. . . .
This Machiavel is one the world can buy,
our world, no slave to strict mechanics, bound
by secret wisdom to a higher fission. . . .
These held us to the rough these twenty years,
unchanging since there was no salad in change;
where is the stink of the coverts where we hid?
The mower starts clanking, daybreak stops the ocean.

10 Sacrificial Killing

All's somewhere, somewhere, thought beats stupidly,
this whole week gone in hunting down the scene—
is it my imagination or
a scarlet patch of Tacitus or Bible,
Pound's Cantos lost in the rockslide of history?
That greatness fled its greatness, fugitive husk
of Cicero without his consular toga,
old sheep sent out to bite the frosty stubble.
This has been going through me for a week.
The scraggly deaf greatness is in his den,
chatting as host on his sofa of magazines,

the youth corps of police stand by him winking . . .
he minds his hands shaking, his hands keep shaking;
if infirmity has a color, it isn't yellow.

11 *For Eugene McCarthy*

I love you so. . . . Gone? Who will swear you wouldn't
have done good to the country, that fulfillment wouldn't
have done good to you—the father, as Freud says:
you? We've so little faith that anyone
ever makes anything better—the same and less—
or that ambition ever makes the ambitious;
the state lifts us, we cannot change the state—all
was yours though, lining down the balls for hours,
freedom in the hollow bowling-alley:
crack of the globe, the boys. . . . Picking a quarrel
with you is like picking the petals of the daisies—
the game, the passing crowds, the rapid young
still brand your hand with sunflecks . . . coldly willing
to smash the ball past those who bought the park.

July 6, 1968

12 *The Immortals*

(FOR MARY MCCARTHY)

'Dear Mary, with her usual motherly
solicitude for the lost overdog. . . .'
But you've always wished to stand by a white horse,
a Jeanne d'Arc by Albrecht Dürer, armed and lettered
in the tougher university of the world. . . .
Since your travels, the horse is firmly there;
you stare off airily into the mundane gossip,
our still more mundane ethics, listen puzzled,
take note; once or twice, blurt your ice-clear sentence—

one hand, for solace, braided in the horse's mane. . . .
The immortals are all about us and below us;
for us *immortal* means another book;
there are too many . . . with us, the music stops;
the first violin stops to wipe the sweat from his bow.

13 For Harpo Marx

Harpo Marx, your hand white-feathered the harp—
the only words you ever spoke were sound.
The movie's not always the sick man of the arts,
yours touched the stars; Harpo, your changing picture
is an unchanging still life, not nature dead.
You dumbly memorized an unwritten script. . . .
I saw you first two years before you died,
near Fifth in Central Park, in fragile autumn:
old blond hair too blonder, old eyes too young.
Two movie trucks and five police lay spoke-wheel
like the covered wagon. The crowd as much or little.
I wish I had knelt; I age to your wincing smile—
Dante's movies, his groups of pain and motion;
the genus *happy* is one generic actor.

14 Assassin!

(From *Les Enfants du Paradis*)
The swinging of a bush, a bird, a fly,
even the shadow of these grown animate,
if anyone really wants to kill anyone. . . .
He waits. He waits. *I am a writer not a leader.*
Even paranoids can have enemies. . . .
A hero might break his spine to better purpose,
like the two *apaches* in *Children of Paradise*,
who ambush the Baron bathing in his bath-house.

No fair play. The Baron (naked) sucks his hookah.
The first killer walks through the screen to his dark game;
the second waits. It's the waiting; which isn't screened!
The last shot: a dead arm hanging from the tub,
the assassin snaps and pockets the bowl of the hookah,
to prove in detachment, perhaps, that something gave.

15 Milton in Separation

It was no loss to the cool and Christian Homer,
blind, cradled in his chair of work, pronouncing
divorce and *marriage* with hard, sardonic R's.
Through the blank dawn of separation, he learned
he only cared for life in the straits. Her flight
put a live elbow in his marble Eve;
she filled the thirst for emptiness—
they struck and then fell hookloose from the fireflesh. . . .
Live-cold in some Greenland on the globe's eyebrow,
free now to study what wooed you most, your writing,
your overobsession posterity must pay. . . .
The pure skim milk of your study is blue to blindness;
the goldfinch flame through the tinderbush. You wished
to set the woods on fire and melt the glacier.

16 The Bond

Once the stoneaxe surrenders its Celt soul,
most civilized marriage honors the day of give-out,
four legs at Bible lengthen out the loveseat—
you and I are returning to the Great War. . . .
From the womb, I say, I scorned Leviathan,
found my intemperate, apocalyptic terms,
host to ten thousand ethnic sovereignties stuck
with their traditional unintelligible tongues . . .

A twenty years of fractious will and feather,
all for goodness, we both on in years,
and the stars in their courses war against us. . . .
Do we love it? It's not returnable;
and what's wrong with living in the greatest city?
Life saves us from dying into truth.

17 Wall-Mirror

(TO CAROLINE)

Moonshine to say we can relive our lives,
begging nature's clean-edge Roman roads
turn back full circle . . . from the byways of night,
day, seeing nothing, missing nothing, God. . . .
The paintings blow over the floor, crack and are free,
blown with the artist who gave them a color.
Your wall-mirror in a mat of plateglass sapphire,
mirror-scroll and claspleaves, holds our faces,
the style and the sitters dead like their portrait, unlearning.
Summer already looks further along than it is,
leaf blighted by streetdyes and the discard girl.
We are on the astigmatic crossroads. One summer, another—
and this one that. You. One life for our two lives—
we stop uncomfortable, we are humanly low.

18 Stalin

Winds on the stems make them creak like things made by man;
a hedge of vines and bushes—three or four
kinds, grape leaf, elephant ear and alder,
an arabesque, imperfect and alive,
a hundred hues of green, the darkest shades
short of black, the palest leaf-backs far from white.
The state, if we could see behind the walls,
is woven of perishable vegetation.

207

Stalin? What shot him clawing up the tree of power—
millions plowed under like the crops they grew,
his intimates dying like the spider-bridegroom?
The large stomach could only chew success. What raised him
was the usual lust to break the icon,
joke cruelly, seriously, and be himself.

Eight Months Later

1 Eight Months Later

It's certain we burned the grass, the grass is burning:
the dismal stones of the field make off for the pond;
safe in the muddy water, they change to ducks
in brown fatigues, eight ducks without a drake—
if we lose the war eight women without a man. . . .
The cement mixer sings like a choir of locusts.
The worst of Manhattan is everything is stacked:
ten buildings dancing in the hat of one,
here a rugged one-family 1890's chateau—
one family? This would house all the first Mormons,
their *droit de seigneur*. One tower would tent Mohammed,
another Abraham. We wish we were elsewhere:
Mexico . . . Mexico? Where is Mexico?
Who will live this year back, cat on the ladder?

2 Die Gold-Orangen

We see the country where the lemon blossoms,
and the pig-gold orange glows on its dark branch,
and the south wind stutters from the blue hustings;
the bluebell is brown, the cypress points too straight—
we see it; it's behind us, love, behind us.
Do you see the house, the roof on marble pillars?
The sideboard silvers, and the arbors blaze;
the statue stands naked to stare at you.
What have I done with us, and what was done?
And the mountain, El Volcán, the climb of clouds?
The mule-man lost his footing in the clouds,

seed of the dragon coupled in the caves. . . .
The cliff drops; over it, the water drops,
and steams away the marks that led us on.

3 *Volveran*

The dark swallows will doubtless come back here killing
the injudicious nightflies with a clack of the beak;
but these that stopped in flight to see your beauty
and my good fortune . . . as if they knew our names—
they'll not come back. The thick lemony honeysuckle,
climbing from its earthroot to your window,
will open more beautiful blossoms to the evening;
but these . . . dewdrops, trembling, shining, falling,
the tears of the day—they'll not come back.
Yet love will sound its fireword to you, and
wake your heart, perhaps, from its deep sleep;
but silent, absorbed, and on their knees,
as men adore God at the altar, as I love you—
don't be deceived, you will not be loved like that.

We Do What We Are

1 The Nihilist as Hero

'All our French poets can turn an inspired line,
but which has written six passable in sequence?'
said Valéry. That was a happy day for Satan. . . .
One wants words meat-hooked from the living steer,
but the cold flame of tinfoil licks the metal log,
the beautifully unchanging fire of childhood
betraying a monotony of vision.
Life by definition breeds on change,
each season we scrap new cars and wars and women.
Sometimes when I am ill or delicate,
the pinched flame of my match turns living green,
the cornstalk in green tails and seeded tassel. . . .
A nihilist has to live in the world as is,
gazing the impossible summit to rubble.

2 Grave Guild

Six poets at a table in the Plaza's ball-and-game-room,
bright as a Viking ship the Dark Age shields,
a forged, eclectic conglomerate of our dreams.
Six hands on the dusty bust of the microphone—
Charlemagne who loved his three R's feared the future,
when he saw the first Normans float out on the Rhine.
Six skulls, the best minds of my generation,
coiffure as out of style as what we write;
six hands on the dusty bust of the microphone:
'Read us your great collage, or something old,
since nothing dead is alien to our tongue.'

I read (a weathercock learns to face both ways)
by some oversight not a word is I:
two O's for eyes in an O for the face of I . . . .

3 Gap

I remember watching old Marshals Joffre and Foche
chauffeured in Roman triumph, though French, through
  Boston;
whatever object I looked at I became—
highschool yellow, nighthawk blue of patrols,
commoner out on saunter with stick and pistol;
I stop the unhurried, hear old Walt Whitman
saying, 'If you'll lend me a dollar, you will help
immortality to stumble on.'
I wish to live my life back to twenty-one,
be ill-at-ease again as everyone,
go a-whoring and a-wandering—
love, a place with a lock and twenty classics.
My wooing at fifty would engulf the siren,
she sings the cure of Kill-river, its bright flow.

4 In the Back Stacks

(PUBLICATION DAY)

My lines swell up and spank like the bow of a yacht;
outside, the break-through of the Broadway bookstores,
outside, the higher voltage of studenten,
the Revolution seeking her professor. . . .
It's life in death to be typed, bound, delivered,
lie on reserve like the old Boston *British Poets*,
hanged for keeping meter. We were complete with Keats;
the editor saw no need for America,
tongue dead as the Latin of the Americas. . . .

One talked such junk all summer behind the stacks.
Things happened when we were talked out, or the sun went
  out,
lay incommunicado. . . . The anthology holds up
without us, the bronze of Cleopatra's cheeks—
everything printed will come to these back stacks.

5 Reading Myself

Like millions, I took just pride and more than just,
first striking matches that brought my blood to boiling;
I memorized tricks to set the river on fire,
somehow never wrote something to go back to.
Even suppose I had finished with wax flowers
and earned a pass to the minor slopes of Parnassus . . . .
No honeycomb is built without a bee
adding circle to circle, cell to cell,
the wax and honey of a mausoleum—
this round dome proves its maker is alive,
the corpse of such insect lives preserved in honey,
prays that the perishable work live long
enough for the sweet-tooth bear to desecrate—
this open book . . . my open coffin.

Rimbaud and Napoleon III

One said the normal flow of my aesthetic
energies was to use the other direction:
I, Rimbaud, servant of France I saved . . .
I was looking for writing I could trust;
but the man was waxy, he jogged along the fields
flowering, a black cigar between his teeth.
His twenty years orgy had made him drunk,
a hand prepared to stub out liberty.
Liberty jogs on, the man is gone,
he's captured. O what name is quaking on
his lip? What plebescites? What Robespierre?
The shark's eye on the horses at Compère . . .
or watching his cigar blue out in smoke,
soirées at Saint Cloud, the bluer vapor . . .

Circles

1 Homing

(FOR ELIZABETH)

To our 20th. We stand set: two trees, their roots;
sometimes the greenest cracks soonest in this soil,
white shells, dry sand for earth. One form *per sempre*;
ten or fifteen pounds superior, since
the Graces gave their hard gold ring, their fistcuff, *Love*—
crown met by what bypaths! Things cling to the aging:
shellacked Pharaoh has the hair of a young squaw,
orchids smell purer than this live crabgrass.
By setting limits, man has withdrawn from the monsters:
metal rods and then a further metal rod;
boundaries mark-step, they give, they take.
When I show my head by your birdhouse you dive me,
graceful, higher, quicker . . . unsteady swallow. . . .
Who will uproot the truth that cannot change?

2 The Hard Way

(FOR HARRIET)

Don't hate your parents, or your children will hire
unknown men to bury you at your own expense.
Child, forty years younger than mother or father,
who will see the coruscations of your furrow,
adolescence snap the feathered barb,
your destiny written in our hands rewritten? . . .
Under the stars, one sleeps, is freed from household,
tufts of grass and dust and tufts of grass,
night oriented to the star of youth—

215

heaven that held the gaze of Babylon—
by harshness, we won the stars. In backward Maine,
ice goes in season to the tropical,
then the mash freezes back to ice, and then
the ice is broken by another wave.

3 Das ewig Weibliche

Serfs with a finer body and tinier brain—
who asks the swallows to do drudgery,
clean, cook, peck up their ton of dust per diem?
Knock on their homes, they go up tight with fear,
farting about all morning past their young,
small as wasps fuming in their ash-leaf ball.
Nature lives off the life that comes to hand;
yet if we knew and softly felt their being,
wasp, bee and bird might live with us on air;
the boiling yellow-jacket in her sack
of zebra-stripe cut short above the knee
escape . . . the nerve-wrung creatures, wasp, bee and bird,
felons for life or keepers of the cell,
wives in their wooden cribs of seed and feed.

4 Sound Mind, Sound Body

Mens sana? O at last; from twenty years
of the annual mania, thirty of adolescence:
this crown. And I am still *in corpore sano*?
Some mornings now my studies wane by eleven,
afternoons by three. The print, its brain,
clouds in mid-chapter, just as I will go—
two score and ten . . . less than common expectation?
All the new years already last? Old times,
when death was nothing, death the dirty crown

on a sound fingernail—ephemeral,
though avant-garde? Now I can tan on my belly
without impatience, almost hear out old people,
live off the family chronicle—the swallow
scents out the kinship, dares swoop me from her nest.

5 Penelope

Manet's bourgeois husband takes the tiller at Cannes,
the sea is right, the virgin's cocky boater,
naive as the moon, streams with its heartstring ribbons—
as if Ulysses were a Sunday friendship. . . .
'Do clothes make the man, or a man the clothes?'
he whistles, gets no answer, sees the household
include him in its polished hollowness,
cellar, womb and the growths—this master, able
to change a silk purse into a sow's ear,
marching his knife-bright floors for wolftracks, thinking
something like this, or something not like this:
'How many a brave heart broken on monologue
revives on ass, or turns to alcohol.
Is it silk cuts scissors, or scissors silk?'

6 Struggle of Non-Existence

Here on this bank where Darwin found his fair one,
and thirty kinds of weeds of the wood in flower,
and a blue shirt, a blue shirt, and our love-beads
rattling together to show that we were young—
we found the fume-gray thistle far-gone in flower.
God dwells inside us and the plowman worm
working this soil that must have lost much sweetness
when Eden and the funk of Abel taught man
the one thing worse than war is massacre. . . .

Man turns dimwit quicker than the mayfly,
asks sleepless drowsiness, not lucid moments;
the tissue sings to sinew, 'Passerby . . .'
Dying beside you, I feel the live blood simmer
in my palms and my feet, and know I am alive.

7 The Spock etc. Sentences

The black hardrubber bathtub stoppers at the Parker House
must have been ordered for their Majesties,
William IV and George IV, then tailored
to the tastes and weight of William Howard Taft.
Things were made right in those days—24-carat
sky over Boston and our first steps to jail.
All night we slept to the sawing of immense
machines constructing: saws in circles slicing
white crescents, shafts and blocks, as if the scheming
intellectuals had rebuilt Tyre and Sidon *ab ovo*—
far from our treasonable, reasonable taunts to save the country,
soft conventions of discourse with lawyers, judge and jury;
'We have had all we can have, and have ruined
so much we cannot safely ruin this.'

July 10, 1968

8 The Good Life

To see the trees flower, and leaves pearl with mist,
fan out above us on the wineglass elms,
life's frills and the pith of life: wife, child and house;
decomposition burning out in service . . .
not ass-licking for medals on the peacock lawn,
tossing birdseed to the blooded gamecock,
vomiting purple in a bullring of slaves—
the Rome of Titus, dull, martyred, and anxious to please.

Fresh legions and old religions hold the eagle.
Freemen might wonder how the imperial tackle,
seldom pleasant and a flail of gallstone,
keeps dragging out the otherwise forgotten,
the sleeping dog, the hero hired for terror,
pearls for the necklace, teeth for the clinking chain.

9 *Trunks*

Tree-worms beam bright white gray in the night;
inside a truck-shed, old tires are hung like paintings. . . .
We say, 'Everyone accepts our claim to greatness,
our best photographers dare not retouch us.
If blood doesn't spurt from our eyelashes, when we meet
a work of art, it isn't art.' In schemes,
too far is easy, enough a miracle;
yet God is good, he sees us all as straw dogs.
Even the toothless, trodden worm can writhe—
in the night-moment, even the halt-pacifist,
nursed on straws and wheat-germ, hears the drum-step
of his kind whistle like geese in converging lines,
hears the police weep in their fog of Mace,
while he plants the black flag of anarchy and peace.

10 *The* Vague, *the Vogue*

Our *New York Times Cookbook* looks like *Leaves of Grass*—
gold title on green. I have escaped its death,
take my two eggs with butter, drink and smoke.
I live past prudence. This is common good
usage. But who can drink the shifting cloud,
lie in small-talk, and tell the truth in print,
be Iago offstage, or Lincoln out of office?
The *vague*, the vogue, what do they tell the critic?

Beethoven's themes are Romantic, but too good:
the republic, death to kings, the living God,
Napoleon. He was his own Napoleon—
for a good talker, hearing is a torture.
Was the captive chorus of *Fidelio* bound?
Does the painted soldier in the painting bleed?

11 *For Archie Smith: 1917-1935*
(*Killed in a car wreck*)

Our sick elms rise to breathe the peace of heaven,
at six the blighted leaves are green as mint,
and the trees' shadows black as trunk or branch—
square white frame and shingled mansard mansion,
building from Jefferson to Warren Harding.
Life's slow. America's ghastly innocence.
One must dream of a summer without a Sunday,
its steerage drive to church, then to Blue Hill. . . .
I have driven when I ought not to have driven.
When cars were horse and buggy and roads dirt,
Smith made Sarasota from Princeton in three days.
A good fast driver is like the Lord unsleeping,
he never kills and he is never killed;
when he dies, someone else is always driving.

12 *The Revolution*

The roadside browns and feeling grows occult,
the terror of spending a summer with a child,
the revolution has happened in the mind,
a fear of moving—when the soul, even the soul
of ruin, leaves a country, the country dies. . . .
'We're in a prerevolutionary situation
at Berkeley, an incredible, refreshing relief

from the rather hot-house, good prep-school sanctum at
  Harvard.
The main thing is our exposure to politics;
whether this *in posse* will determine
these revolutionaries' slaughter in the streets,
la guerra civile, I don't know.
Anyway you should be in on it. Only
in imagination can we lose the battle.'

13 *Youth*

They go into the world, innocent, wordy, called
in too many directions I would like to go,
stretching out their 20's to 2000.
When I was young and farther from the young
half my friends were writers, half my girlfriends
had already read the news when I was born,
they read that kings must either reign or die.
Many a youth will turn from student to tiger,
revolutionaries will sleep in the grave,
blasphemous, unavoidable—the Mother,
known in our slow, cold debaucheries,
the bitter, dry pelt of feline undulation,
weeps by her door of colored beads, and holds
youth old as Michelangelo to her bosom.

14 *River Harbor*

I sit here seeing some recorded harbor,
wilds fitting our first Academy's pomp of youth,
or Aaron Burr's flirtations with frontiers. . . .
We're warpage in the drift to *fin de siècle*,
your sawdust wharfpiles running a third of a mile:
up river, up river, and none will go to town.

Old rot without a burden! Your house is a cookie-box,
small costly motors moving small battery-sculptures;
the only art is amusement. Rib of your father,
child drowning the summer in puzzles, in shady tennis:
all visible for a fling of fifty miles
from Stonington to Mount Desert to Bangor;
we lying under glass in a greenhouse at noon . . .
The structures rise from water and tower in air.

15 *Shipwreck Party*

Ethics meant government, the civil service,
the Prussian school, the Irish patrol, and now
those long steel scoopnets lie rolled in the bureau;
at night we listen to the great debate,
hardware exploding its help on the city poor.
Not our game; we, dead cells demagnetized. . . .
You puzzle out small devices fine as motors,
set the children and parents dancing in costume,
dance dressed as a beercan, crosscut, zany thing—
joy and enough disorder for a country night.
After the party, we hear the unthrottled car
looping the town, a runner panting his jog,
many laps in no time . . . a town is small—
none too small to take power, split hairs with a mallet.

16 *Playing the* Archduke Trio

Who marched in the Archduke's War or worse lost cause,
without promise of plunder, murder and gallantry?
Marriage can't be less ruffian than this:
needlehead pillow-pillow to needlehead,
long drowning, a toe just skating the flint of bottom.
This bright night the heavens mackerel in my garden—

cloud-flesh of the turtle given shape by shell,
Aphrodite fleeing her man's cowed rib,
forsaking father, mother, love, friends for bondage.
I so pray this pretty sky to stay:
peace to cool blood, and peace to this cold dew,
elms black on the moon, our birdhouse on a pipe. . . .
Beethoven's Archduke was a poor man . . . Beethoven
betrothed to the single muse, her ear of flint.

17 High Blood

I watch my blood pumped into crystal pipes,
red sticks like ladycrackers for a child—
nine-tenths of me, and yet it's lousy stuff.
Touched, it stains, slips, drips, sticks; and it's lukewarm.
All else—the brains, the bones, the stones, the soul—
is peripheral flotsam on this live flow.
On my great days of sickness, I was God—
my flesh shimmers, I catpad on my blood,
the universe moves beneath me when I move.
It's the aorta and heartbeat of my life;
acid rock turned high, teen-age record purring,
as if we stuck a cat with a diamond needle—
cry of high blood for blood that gives both tyrant
and tyrannized their short half-holiday.

18 The Lost Tune

As I grow older, I must admit with terror:
I have been there, the masterwork has lost,
music that taught, philosophies that danced.
Their *vivace* clogs, I am too wise, or tired.
One learns from books that even woman dies;
most women hold up longer than a landscape—

yours were New Hampshire, engraved in black and white
to better show the formal luxury of
a million trees and creepers marching up
the flank of a cliff, microscopes on each leaf;
below, your weaponed huntress hunts her huntsman,
the lover panting to her stag at bay;
not very true, yet art—had Schubert sung it, risen
from the Vienna greenroom to this death.

19 Death and the Maiden

In Romantic painting, the girl is Body,
just as to die she must embody youth;
Death too must take on body to make a scene—
Verismo is no *vehicle* for Death.
And in music . . . I have been thirty years
deciphering themes in Schubert's *Death and the Maiden*;
a person dying is death's own impersonation,
Schubert dying is audible; yet Death,
if anything, is melodrama; Death
quickly drops his actors for the living. . . .
Years of dead friends, still mine—what other possession
allows no aging or devaluation?
A good ear hears its own death talking—*only
in art or the movies can the maiden live.*

20 Heat

For the first time in fifteen years, a furnace
Maine night that would have made summer anywhere,
in Arizona. The wooden rooms of our house
dry, redoubling their wooden farmhouse smell,
honest wooden ovens shaking with desire.
We feared the pressure might be too curative.

Outside, a young seal festered on the beach,
head snapped off, the color of a pig;
much lonelier, this formula for cures.
One nostril shut, my other attenuated—
it's strange tonight to want to teach and pencil
reminders on bits of paper, 'I must remember
to breathe through my mouth. Breathe from your mouth,'
as the mouth kept closing on the breath of morning.

Grasshoppers

(TO STANLEY KUNITZ)

Who else grew up in the shadow of Worcester, Mass?
Why do we wake from a ten second sleep
half-lifeless? The concerto still andante;
I, held back in my allwhiteboy boarding school,
class of '35 whittling '35;
the pre-Prohibition summer cottages,
one white eastern exposure—in the yard,
hand-made cases for fled skunk and turtle,
lost generation sunset, its big red rose
for the long, silent dinners when no-one talked.
Always the sound thirty-five years we've lost;
years for our versing and our years with children.
We say the blades of grass are hay. We sing
the Joyful the creatures find no word to sing.

The Races

1 August

This night the mustard bush and goldenrod
and more unlikely yellows tread a spiral,
blue china snakes, blue ribbons—cool not cold,
the vase eviscerated down to ribbon. . . .
Brotherly, stacked and mean, the great Convention
throws out its Americana like dead flowers:
choices, at best, that cannot hurt, or cure;
many are chosen, and so few were called. . . .
And yet again, I see the yellow bush rise,
formations, I suppose, beyond the easel;
one summer, two summers, young breasts escape the rib;
the future is only standing on our feet,
and what can be is only what will be—
the sun warms the mortician, unpolluted.

August 7, 1968

2 Five-Hour Rally

All excel, as if they were the candidate,
first of the twenty first-ballerinas in the act,
all original or at least in person. . . .
Many sunsets are printed on the acre rug,
one figure to each ten feet, like the rich in his grave;
its head is a broken pretzel, less head than gulf;
the wings are fernshoots, done like ironwork
for a Goya balcony, lure and bar to love.
But the belly is a big watermelon seed,
the body is the belly's overcoat—

227

wormseed, it could only live for that. . . .
Sunrise breaks. Who can live on breath alone?
Insects and statesmen grapple on the carpet,
saying, 'You will swallow me. I you.'

3 The Flaw

The old flaw in my eye is sprouting bits and strings
gliding like dragon-kites in the Chinese sky;
I was afraid to look more closely, and count—
today I am too exhausted to be afraid,
I gaze in the white-cloud window of my plane,
see in it my many flaws are still one,
a flaw with a tail the color of shed skin,
inaudible rattle of the rattler's disks.
God is design, this ugliness confides
the goodness of His will, and gives me warning—
the scrape of the Thunderer's fingernail. . . .
Faust's soul-sale was for life to do his work;
yet death is sweet now, weariness almost lets
me taste its sweetness none will ever taste.

4 Fear in Chicago

The little millionaire's place, sheen of the centuries;
as my eye roved, everything freshly French;
then I saw a score marked *sans rigueur*
on the little grand piano, muddy white,
a blank white and medallion-little bust
of Franz Schubert, a blown-up colored photograph
of the owner's wife, executive-Bronzino—
this frantic touch of effort! Or out-window,
two cunning cylinder skyscraper apartment buildings—
six circles of car garage below the homes,

moored boats below the cars—more Louis Quinze
and right than anything in this apartment;
except the little girl's bedroom, perfect with posters:
'Do not enter,' and 'Sock it to me, Baby.'

August 26, 1968

5 'We Are Here to Preserve Disorder'

The beefy door ajar an inch or two,
the green screen seeing more than if I'd seen it . . .
I saw a dark strip of silenced stalk in rippling,
the singed back of a Burmese cat that crashed my gate—
non-verbal Cordelia, the wordless voice of Chicago.
Some cats are persons . . . mine packed and left a bottle:
'R. LOWELL: for nervousness, Dr. Baumann.'
The police weren't baby-sitting at 5 A.M.;
in our staff headquarters, three heads smashed, one club.
For five days the Hilton was liberated by cops and troops—
fall of a government. The youth for McCarthy
knew and blew too much on their children's crusade.
Our waste fell from the windows at the end of the party. . . .
'How can you have a Convention if you can't throw out
a beercan?'

6 After the Convention

Life, hope, they conquer death, generally, always;
and if the steamroller goes over the flower, the flower dies.
Some are more solid earth; they stood in lines,
blouse and helmet, a creamy de luxe sky-blue—
the music, savage and ephemeral. . . .
After five nights of Chicago: police and mob,
I am so tired and had, clichés are wisdom,
the clichés of paranoia. On this shore,

229

the fall of the high tide waves is a straggling, joshing
march of soldiers . . . on the march for me. . . .
How slender and graceful, the double line of trees,
how slender, graceful, irregular and underweight,
the young in black folk-fire circles below the trees—
under their shadow, the green grass turns to hay.

September 1, 1968

7 The Hospital

We're lost here if we follow what we read,
worse lost if hearsay is our common voice;
we need courses in life and life, and what's alive;
trips to the hospital. . . . One has seen stiffs
that look alive, they mostly look alive,
twitched by green fingers till they turn to flowers;
they are and are not—some poor candidate,
stone-deaf ear no felon's sledge will wake. . . .
Others are strapped to their cots, thrust out in hallways,
browner, dirtier, flatter than the dead leaves,
they are whatever crinkles, plugged to tubes,
and plugged to jugs of dim blue doctored water,
held feet above them to lift the eye to heaven—
these look dead, unlike the others, they are alive.

8 Forethought

(FOR HARRIET)

I dream a kind of camp army, not altogether
anything from Chicago, has barbwired off
my house. I wake up, shouting, 'No, don't, don't!'
I seize hold of my consciousness, prove myself
but half awake, run the doubtful parallel
between having life and the moment just now gone. . . .

To live long enough to see our children live:
this has been worked out before, is current.
You are too young to wish us otherwise,
too thoughtful ever to wish us wholly other;
yet to see you happy would mean to lead
your life for you, hold hard, and live you out.
It doesn't go this way; this doesn't go—
so calm, perhaps, will be the final change.

September 4, 1968

9 November 6

Election Night, the last Election Night,
without drink, television or a friend—
wearing my dark blue knitted tie to classes. . . .
No one has recognized that blue meant black.
My daughter telephones me from New York,
she talks *New Statesman*, 'Then we're cop-outs! Isn't
not voting Humphrey a vote for Nixon and Wallace?'
And I, 'Not voting Nixon is my vote for Humphrey.'
It's funny-awkward; I don't come off too well;
'You mustn't tease me, we were clubbed in Chicago.'
We must rouse our broken forces and save the country:
we often said this, now the beaten player
opens old wounds and hungers for the blood-feud
hidden like contraband and loved like whiskey.

10 November 7: From the Painter's Loft

The wet bare tar, the same Back Bay station;
most of Boston is now a builders' project,
blank and unspoiled and white. Here nothing's slid
since 1925. The Prudential Building
that raised and saved the skyline, here saves nothing;

paperweight, removable plug-in. We can
still gulp Bohemia with the boorishness of boys
from this window, and see the *Thread and Needle Shoppe*,
where we stole a fifteen-dollar microscope,
then tried to make them pay back fifteen dollars. . . .
Nobody has won, nobody has lost;
on the broad tar, the starry headlights twinkle
from Portland, Maine to Portland, Oregon.
Will the election-winners ever pay us back?

Winter

In his dark day, Dante made the mistake of treating
politics as if it belonged to life,
not ideology. In Purgatory,
the poor souls eclipse the black and white of God.
Likeness to exile warms the sun in Hell—
the man running for his life never tires:
Ser Brunetto, running like one of those
who ran for the green cloth through the green fields
at Verona, looks like the one who won
the roll of cloth, not like those who lose. . . .
All comes from a girl met at the wrong time:
God and her love that called him forth to exile
in midwintertime cold and lengthening days,
when the brief field frost mimics her sister, snow.

Four Poems for Elizabeth Bishop

1 Water 1948

Stonington: each morning boatloads of hands
cruised off for the granite quarry on an island;
they left dozens of bleak white frame houses stuck
like oyster shells on the hill of rock. Remember?
We sat on the slab of rock. From this distance in time,
it seems the color of iris, rotting and turning purpler,
but it was only the usual gray rock
turning fresh green when drenched by the sea.
The sea flaked the rock at our feet, kept lapping the
    matchstick
mazes of weirs where the fish for bait were trapped.
You dreamed you were a mermaid clinging to a wharfpile,
trying to pull off the barnacles with your hands.
We wished our two souls might return like gulls to the rock.
In the end, the water was too cold for us.

2 Flying from Bangor to Rio 1957

A twelve-foot cedar hedge screens out the human,
teenage softball makes the Castine Common
a *Youth's Companion* cover. North & south
from Halifax to Rio the same Atlantic—
you can never settle on where to be,
lashed by your giant memory to the globe.
Canada's Georges rule your horoscope;
long, long, may mad King George in cap and bells
sway over your Nova Scotia, nowhere else—
a whitebeard, deaf, blind, singing Church of England

hymns he accompanied on his harpsichord.
You wished you were a horse, some South Italian
sitting at your own bar in Greenwich Village,
standing drinks for relations who never go outdoors.

3 Letter with Poems for a Letter with Poems

'You're right to worry about me, only please DON'T,
though I'm pretty worried myself. I've somehow got
into the worst situation I've ever
had to cope with. I can't see the way out.
Cal . . . have you ever gone through caves?
I did once . . . Mexico, and hated it—
I've never done the famous ones near here.
Finally after hours of stumbling along,
one sees daylight ahead, a faint blue glimmer.
Air never looked so beautiful before.
That's what I feel I'm waiting for now:
a faintest glimmer I am going to get out
somehow alive from this. Your last letter helped,
like being handed a lantern or a spiked stick.'

4 Calling 1970

The new painting has to live on iron rations,
rush brushstroke, indestructible technique,
French *plein air* to cloak austerity.
Albert Ryder left his crackled amber moonscape
to ripen in sunlight. His painting was repainting,
his tiniest work weighs heavy in the hand.
Who is killed if the horseman never cry halt?
Have you ever seen an inchworm crawl on a leaf,
cling to the very end, revolve in air,
feeling for something to reach something? Do

you still hang words in air, ten years imperfect,
joke-letters, glued to cardboard posters, with gaps
and empties for the unimagined phrase,
unerring Muse who scorns a less casual friendships?

America from Oxford
(*May 5, 1970*)

The cattle has stopped in the Godstow meadow,
a peacock wheels his tail to move the heat,
then pivots, changing to a wicker chair,
tiara of thistle on his shitty bobtail.
It's the feathery May and England, but the heat
is American summer. Two weeks use up three months;
at home, the colleges are closed for summer,
the students march . . . *Brassman* lances Cambodia,
he has lost his pen, the sword folds in his hand like felt—
Is truth here with you, if I sleep well,
Bystander? The peacock spins, the Revolution
hasn't involved us . . . a heat that moves
air so estranged and hot I might be home. . . .
We have climbed above the wind to breathe.

Summer

1 These Winds

(FOR HARRIET)

I see these winds, these are the tops of trees,
these are no heavier than green alder bushes;
touched by a light wind, they begin to mingle
and race for instability—too high placed
to last a day in the brush, these are the winds. . . .
Downstairs, you correct notes at the upright piano,
doubly upright this midday torn from the whole
green cloth of summer; your room is dark as a cloakroom,
the loose tap beats time, you hammer the formidable
chords of *The Nocturne*, your second composition.
Since you first began to bawl and crawl
from sheltered lawn to this shady room, how often
these winds have crossed the wind of inspiration—
in these too, the unreliable touch of the all.

2 Glass for Our Wedding Anniversary

Jade leaves espaliered on our barn's top window,
sky stretched on the two-pane sash . . . it doesn't open:
thud of roofdrip, this leaf or that leaf twings
to the needle-heaven the heartless leaf rejects—
the blight's green-inked, a picture to sell for money.
In Chardin's still, the paint runs, juice is moving—
two to twenty years to live beyond our means,
art a frame to hold and veins to bleed,
we hardly the first cripple to place in the race.
Often the player's outdistanced by the game;

Kant, Jane Austen stayed unmarried and sane.
This week our first this season to go unfretted;
a house eats up the wood that made it—our bodies
smelling green as the weeds that bruise the grass.

July 28

3 La Condition Humaine

(FOR HARRIET)

Should someone human, not just our machinery
firing on its fling, do for the world and us,
surely they'll say he chose the lesser evil;
our wars were better than their marriages,
ape on she-ape boozing down Saturday night—
home things can't stand up to the strain of the earth.
Now when I wake to their airs of steaks and Charles Ives;
the regional classic lifts my fell of hair—
David once lulled the dark nucleus of Saul—
as you at twelve must, at twenty, fifty, ninety,
young in a century that has lost my name;
no date I wish you could be long enough,
if possibility were tied to fact—
only acid shellfish fear fresh air.

4 End of Camp Alamoosook

Less than a score, the dregs of the last day,
counselors and campers, man the last cove of island;
the unexpected, the exotic, the early
morning sunlight is more like premature twilight:
last day of the day, foreclosure of the camp.
Glare on the amber squatters, fire of fool's-gold—
like bits of colored glass, it cannot burn.
The Acadians must have gathered in such arcs;

my cousin herded them from Nova Scotia—
no malice, merely working in his line of work,
herding guerrillas in some Morality.
Order! The campers harden in their shyness,
their gruff, faint voices hardly say hello,
crying, 'Do we love it? *We love it.*'

5 Familiar Quotations

(FOR HARRIET)

The poet then, if all else fail, his words from nowhere:
near the ocean, skipping five smooth stones—too happy,
sometimes the little muddler can't stand itself. . . .
Her transistor is singing Anton Webern;
say what it's like? It's hard; if you'll listen to this,
you can listen to anything—it's like red ants,
wild ants, the wild wolf through the woods walking;
wild spiders crying together without tears. . . .
Not this; we want the truth, the very Truth:
he imagined all men were his soul-brother,
Pharisees boiled him in his bloody sweat;
he was all men, he was you, he might have lived;
for love, he threw his lovely youth away—
but you can't love everyone, your heart won't let you.

6 Mink

In the unspoiled age, when they caught a cow-mink,
they made her urinate around the traps,
and every bull-mink hunting along the stream
fell in the trap, and soon the mink were done—
the last we heard of was a freeze in the 50's,
the last bull making tracks in the snow for a last cow.
My friend, once professional, no longer traps:

'We've too many ways to make a living now'—
his a G.I. pension, and two working sons.
He builds houses for bluebirds, martins and swallows.
When a pair mates in one, it's like a catch,
like trapping something—he's sent, it's like a conversion,
China's lost hope to excel without improving. . . .
His money goes to *Wildlife*; he killed too much.

7 Cattle

The moon, invisible behind a cloud-ledge,
briefly douses its bonfire on the harbor. . . .
Machiavelli despised these furiously fought
mounted Tuscan mercenary battles:
lines rushed, and Greek met Greek; one man was killed,
men died of a stroke, but not the strokes of battle.
Our police hit more to terrorize than kill:
a hundred riots, nobody left dead;
clubs broken and brains, women dissolved on the line—
none distorted forever. Cattle have guts,
screwed, they live for it as much as we,
a one-week mother, then working mothers; the calf
goes into the calfpool; but after the barn is burned,
they will look at the sunset and tremble.

8 The Going Generation

Our going generation; there are days
of pardon . . . perhaps to go on living in
the old United States of William James,
its plaintive, now arthritic, optimism—
hear the swallow's coloratura cheep and cluck,
shrilling underneath its racket, *fuck*;
the feeder dealing out his catfood like cards

to yearling salmon in their stockpond by the falls.
Grace-days . . . it is less than heaven, this dwindling
bulkhead of lawn black with binoculars,
overlooking the moon and ocean rising . . .
earth an eyelash on the lens—drink, drink, see,
the rings of Saturn horseshoe round the light-globe. . . .
Some alternatives have no answer; time must answer.

9 Bringing a Turtle Home

On a torrent highway, we spotted a domed stone,
a painted turtle turned to stone by fear.
I picked it up. The turtle had come a long walk,
200 millenia understudy to dinosaurs,
then their survivor. A god for the out-of-power. . . .
We have our faster gods, flush yachtsmen who see
hell as a city very much like New York,
these gods give a bad past and worse future to men
who never bother to set a spinnaker;
culture without cash isn't worth their spit.
The laughter on Mount Olympus was always breezy. . . .
Goodnight, little Boy, little Soldier, live,
a toy to your friend, a stone of stumbling to gods—
sandpaper Turtle, scratching your pail for water.

10 Returning Turtle

A week slogging the road, one fasting in the bathtub,
raw hamburger mossing in the watery stoppage,
the room drenched with musk like kerosene—
no one shaved, and only the turtle washed.
He was so beautiful when we flipped him over:
greens, reds, yellows, fringe of the shadowy savage,
the last Sioux grown old and wise, saying with weariness,

'Why doesn't the Great White Father put his red
children on wheels, and move us as he will?'
We drove to the Orland River, and watched the turtle
rush for water like rushing into marriage,
swimming his uncontaminated joy,
lovely the flies that fed that sleazy surface,
a turtle looking back at us, and blinking.

11 The Stump and Green Shoots

'Cousin Cal—your Liz is from middle country, Kentucky,
is this strictly the Southern roots of the rose?
My dear, dear Fultons—Auntie (Liz Ross Fulton)
is letting go at ninety-three this August;
Uncle John ate only one bite of roast beef
at his ninetieth birthday dinner last month;
Mother's cataract glasses are good, but she can't
see to paint, she is only eighty-six;
only Aunt Margaret at ninety-five plus
is *indominateable*. Don't worry,
I'm not going to be a poet, I haven't suffered.
I've left the *Savanna Globe*, reporting's not writing;
I've got to write for me. George will support me;
haven't all great artists had their patrons?'

12 Christians

'I want to eat dirt, I want to rub salt in my hurt,'
they cry—O words with heavenly comfort fraught!
And in good conscience, when Christianity
ceases to be a torture-machine, it stops.
I miss the white militia, the last schoolmen's
abstract-expressionist image of the saved,
David and Bathsheba who used to tell me,

'If you stepped on a thumbtack each time you went to a
    woman. . . .'
Each word's a scissors cutting my brother's throat.
It's this waking daily to the fire of daybreak:
a hurt mother sleeps awake like a cat till daybreak,
sleeps on the mat by the bed of our breathy child—
her cat thrusts its small brown arm thru the crack in the door,
another arm, a brown nose, and the door sticks.

13 Nesting

Discovering, discovering trees are green at night,
braking headlights-down, ransacking the roadside
for someone strolling, fleeing to her wide goal;
passing blanks, the white Unitarian Church,
dark barn on my bulwark, two scowling unlit shacks,
the town pool just drained, the white lighthouse unplugged,
watching the beerfroth on the muddy breakers,
dwarfed by the STATE OF MAINE, white iceberg at drydock.
The question, my questioners? It's not for them—
crouched in the gelid drip of the pine in our garden,
invisible even when found, till we toss a white raincoat
over your sky-black, blood-trim quilted stormcoat—
you saying *I would prefer not*, like Bartleby:
small deer tremble and steely in wet nest!

14 No Hearing

Belief in God is an inclination to listen,
but as we grow older and our freedom hardens,
we hardly even want to hear ourselves,
the silent universe is auditor. . . .
I am to myself, my trouble sings,
the highway shines to Bangor, the usual autumn

flight of Canada geese V above it, moonborne,
the path too certain; Dante found this path
even before the first young leaves turned green,
stark seniority that spined his youth. . . .
White side, black window, white side, black window, white
    side,
my empty house . . . in the garden, pine dip, stand straight;
I stand face to face with lost ages—my breath
is life, the rough, the smooth, the bright, the drear.

15 Castine Harbor

Mostly it's a color; its change and yield
give easily, no stand except the headland:
one substance everywhere divisible;
bosom of salt, it floats us—less and less
usable now we can fly like the angels.
Yet who would stay alive without the ocean?
Shall we boast marriage is like the ocean:
two parts hydrogen nagging for oxygen—
as if the formula existed everywhere
in the numinous Parnassus of chemistry?
The statesman mutters, 'The problems of politics
are nothing. . . .' He was thinking of his marriage—
habitual, changing, the sea is marriage; God is
H_2O Who must forgive us for having lived.

16 Castine 1860

One misses Emerson drowned in luminism,
the vast serenity of emptiness,
and Fitz Hugh Lane painting a ship moored in Castine
within shouting distance of my barn in 1860,
its bright flywings fixed in the topographical

severity of a world reworked as glass.
Tools are honestly made, and often jails;
the horror of top-flight skyscraper villages
is the stench of loneliness they give off—
elemental material, line to line to line,
the skeletal Trinity of Thomas Aquinas.
One should take a notebook into jail,
nothing is real until set down in words—
we are ice returning to water.

17 Joy

On the great day, when the eyelid of life lifts—
why hide it? Joy has had the lion's share;
then, as Ezra Pound said, 'Amy Lowell is
no skeleton to hide in your closet.' Poor flesh—
the red leaves ember in the blue cool of fall,
the hour, the half hour, before the whiskey hooks,
the humor, the loyalty, the seductive verb,
mouth like a twat, vagina like a jaw,
small-mouth bass shaking the treble hooks. . . .
Descending back into *contemptu mundi*,
I sit, stood-up, in the wrong restaurant,
ringing spare change like sleighbells in my pocket,
fulfilling the prophecy of my first prize,
a field cup won for catching snakes and moths.

18 Nature

The circular moon saw-wheels up the oak-grove;
below it, clouds—a permanent of clouds,
many as the waves of the Atlantic, and shingled.
It makes men larger to sleep with the sublime,
the Magna Mater *had*, shivers under oak, moon, cloud.

Such cures the bygone Reichian prophets swore to,
such did as gospel for those virgin times—
two elements were wanting: man and nature.
By sunrise, the show has shifted. Strings of fog,
such as we haven't seen in fifteen months,
catch shyly over lobsterboats and island:
smoke-dust the Chinese draftsman made eternal.
His drawing wears; the hand decayed. A hand does—
we can have faith, at least, the hand decayed.

19 *Growth*

(FOR HARRIET)

'I'm talking the whole idea of life, and boys,
with Mother; and then the heartache, when we're fifty. . . .
You've got to call your next book, *Book of the Century*,
but it will take you a century to write,
then I will have to continue it, when you die.'
Latin, Spanish, swimming half a mile,
writing a saga with a hero named Eric,
Latin, Spanish, math and rollerskates;
a love of pretty dresses, but not boys;
composing something with the bells of *Boris*:
'UNTITLED, would have to be the name of it. . . .'
You grow apace, you grow too fast apace,
too fast adult; no, not adult, mature.
On the telephone, they say, 'We're tired, aren't you?'

20 *The Graduate*

(FOR ELIZABETH)

'Transylvania's Greek Revival Chapel
is one of the best Greek Revival things in the South;
the College's most distinguished graduate

was a naturalist, he had a French name like Audubon.
My sister, Margaret, a one-bounce basketball
player and all-Southern Center, came home
crying each night because of "Happy" Chandler,
the coach, and later Governor of Kentucky.
Our great big tall hillbilly idiots keep
Kentucky pre-eminent in basketball.
All that! Still, if you are somewhat ill-born,
you feel your soul is not quite first-class. . . .'
Never such shimmering of intelligence,
though the wind was short, and you stopped smoking.

21 Outlivers

'If we could slow the world to what it changed
a hundred years ago, or any hundred,
too scrupulous handwork, farmwork, hand-made wars;
God might give us His right to live forever
despite the eroding miracle of science. . . .'
'Was everything that much grander than it is?'
'We think so, but the grandeur dropped us here—
no, it's only people we must miss.
The cave-man, retarded epochs like crab and clam,
wept, as we do, his person dead.' We talk
like room-mates bleeding out night to dawn,
each crowds the others to outlive us all—
'But you and Harriet are perhaps like countries
not yet ripe for self-determination.'

22 My Heavenly Shiner
(FOR ELIZABETH)

The world atop our heads in Maine is north,
zeroes through Newfoundland and Hudson Bay:
entremets chinois et canadiens.

A world like ours will tumble on our heads,
my heavenly Shiner, think of it curving on;
you quiver on my finger like a small
minnow robbed from the shimmer of the globe,
flittering radiance of my flittering finger.
The fish, the shining fish, they go in circles,
not one of them will make it to the Pole—
this isn't the point though, this is not the point;
think of it going on without a life—
in you, God knows, I've had the earthly life—
we were kind of religious, we thought in images.

23 It Did

Knowledge, we've had it; our character, the public's—
and yet we will mature, and know we once
did most things better, not just physical
acts, moral: turning home too high for love,
living twenty-four hours in shirt and drawers,
breathless short hauls, the breathless singles' service;
we could have done much worse. We hope we did
a hundred thousand things much worse! Poor X's,
chance went this way, that way with us here:
gain scored off loss, loss off gain: our tideluck—
it did to live with, but finally all men worsen;
the drone caught up in honey, the saint in blackouts,
old jaw that only smiles to bite the feeder.
Corruption serenades the wilting tissue.

24 Seals

If we must live again, not us; we might
go into seals, we'd handle ourselves better:
able to dawdle, able to torpedo,

all too at home in our double elements,
our third of rocks and ledges—if man were dormant. . . .
We flipper the harbor, blots and patches and oilslick,
so much bluer than water, we think it sky.
Creature could face creator in this suit,
fishers of fish not men. Some other August,
the easy seal might say, 'I could not sleep
last night; suddenly I could write my name.'
Then all seals, preternatural like us,
take direction, head north—their haven
green ice in a greenland never grass.

Father and Sons

1 Michael Tate: August 1967—July 1968

Each night, a star, gold-on-black, a muskellunge,
dies in the highest sphere that never dies. . . .
Things no longer usable for our faith
go on routinely possible in nature;
the worst is the child's death. Even his stone,
the very, very old one, one century, two,
his one-year date common in auld lang syne
is no longer faith's eye-scale. And, Michael Tate,
gagging on your plastic telephone,
while the raw sitter drew water for your bath,
unable to hear your groans. . . . They think: if there'd been
a week or two's illness, we might have been prepared. . . .
Your twin crawls for you, ten-month twin. They are no longer
young enough to understand what happened.

2 Letters from Allen Tate

This winter to watch the child of your old age;
and write, 'He is my captor. As a young man,
I was too alert to let myself enjoy
my daughter's infancy as I do the little boy's.'
Ah that was the mosses ago in your life, mine;
no more eastern flights this season. 'As you must guess,
we're too jittery to travel after Michael's death.'
You are still magisterial and cocky as when
you gave us young romantics your directive,
Shoot when you get the chance, and shoot to kill.'
Who else would sire twin sons at sixty-eight?

How sweet your life in retirement! What better than loving
a young wife and boy; without curses writing,
'I shall not live long enough to "see him through." '

The End

1 Dies Irae, *A Hope*

'The day this day of wrath will do the world,
sings Sibyl on snow, sings David *Guerrillero*,
'the judge is hooded, canaries sing in torture;
God shoot down everything, even what don't move.'
Our God and King of greatest majesty,
you who save those you must save free; you, whose
least anger makes our worst a derelict,
you have descended from the hills for us,
keep walking to and fro on earth for us;
how often seeking us here you are dead! . . .
Everything points to non-existence except existence—
was a day God looked and saw the world was good,
in His hands, God got us in His hands . . .
good reason to pardon us, this time for pardon.

2 *On the Border*

'Is Mao's China nearer to Utopia?'
'Only by twelve or fifteen dynasties;
Mao still thinks it dishonorable to carry
firearms except for the birds, war and mobs.'
'Are we altogether certain of that much here?'
'Mao is Establishment set to go down fanged,
old king-ape of the ape-horde preferring injustice to violence.'
'High culture is lying with an American girl
on the Canadian border, belt of the earth,
each man here noble as the Queen but not so rich.'
None will leave his cell for wife or service.'

'Friends are such a good thing we should cry welcome, welcome, even if they come from hell. . . .'
'There's a strong shadow where there's this much light.'

For John Berryman

I feel I know what you have worked through, you
know what I have worked through—these are words. . . .
John, we used the language as if we made it.
Luck threw up the coin, and the plot swallowed,
monster yawning for its mess of pottage.
Ah privacy, as if you wished to mount
some rock by a mossy stream, and count the sheep—
fame that renews the soul, but not the heart.
The ebb tide flings up wonders: rivers, linguini,
beercans, bloodstreams, eddies; how gaily they gallop
to catch the ocean—Herbert, Thoreau, Pascal,
born to die like athletes in their forties—
Abraham roamed with less expectancy,
heaven his friend, the earth his follower.

Closing

1 Close the Book

The book is finished and the air is lighter,
I recognize the people in the room;
I touch your pictures, find you in the round.
The cat sits pointing the window from the bedspread,
hooked on the nightlife flashing through the curtain;
he is a *dove* and thinks the lights are pigeons—
flames from the open hearth of Thor and Saul,
arms frescoed on the vaults of the creeping cavern,
missiles no dialectician's hand will turn,
fleshspots for the slung chunks of awk and man.
Children have called the anthropoid, father;
he'd stay home Sunday, and they walked on coals. . . .
The passage from lower to upper middle age
is quicker than the sigh of a match in the water—
we too were students, and betrayed our hand.

2 Out of the Picture

Tank. A camel blotting up the water.
God with whom nothing is voulu or design.
The lay-off . . . the Sun-day now all seven, a trek
for the great image held behind Blue Hill,
the flower of Eden unchanged, since spoiled,
the girl holding the sunset apple, lifeclass unchanged . . .
white as a white cake of soap in the dingy bathlight.
Things have been felt before, before today:
the joyless stupor . . . Orpheus in Genesis—
he hashed words from brute sound, he taught his sons English,

plucked all the flowers, deflowered all the girls
with the exaggeration of a Negro,
with too many words. His sons killed and ate him;
we dance round the cookout with festal gaiety.

Half a Century Gone

1

(FOR ELIZABETH)

We can go on, if free to leave the earth;
our blood, too high, resumes the mortal coil,
hoping past hope to round the earth of Greenbeard,
our springtide's circlet of the fickle laurel,
a funeral wreath from the Despotic Gangster.
I feel the woven cycles of His pain,
reticulations of His spawning cells,
the intimations of my family cancer.
With us no husband could sit out the marriage;
those shadowy patriarchs, once gamed like children,
they lacked staying power, not will to live. . . . Dead now,
their relics who kept them living by rushing out
blackbordered letters like stamps from Turkestan.
Where are they? They had horses, the gods of the city. . . .

2

Those serfs with the pageboy bob of Shakespeare's kings,
enameled with joy, or speechless with affliction,
are like this summer's landscape chilling under
the first influence of the evening star,
winking from green to black—the body, black
before we even knew that we were dead.
And neither of us the wiser or kinder—torn
darlings, professional sparring partners; and
but for the impossible love, a loyalty
beyond abasement, outside anywhere:

258

all icy pandemonium. Beatrice
always met me too early or too late,
piercing the firelit hollow of the marriage—
some brightest prong, antennae of the ant. . . .

3

And here on this wavy earth, we, like the others,
too thoughtful clods, may learn from those we walk on:
Star-nosed moles, their catatonic tunnels
and barrows . . . only in touch with what they touch;
blind fur, in mourning, black from shying at limelight,
not as we would, or the lowest serf—
vegetating and protecting creatures,
forever falling short of our shortest life.
Through my fieldglasses, I aggrandize
a half-fledged robin with a speckled breast,
big as a pheasant. . . . The invincible
syllogism advances from talon to talon;
no earthly ripple disturbs the ballbearing
utility of the bald and nearest planet. . . .

4

We will remember then our tougher roots:
forerunners hooped to the broiling soil,
until their backs were branded with the coin
of Alexander, small hexagonal sores—
as if they were stretched on burning chicken wire,
skin cooked red and hard as a rusted tin can
by the footlights of the sun—Tillers of the desert!
Think of them, afraid of violence,
afraid of anything, timid as sheep
hidden in some casual, protective crevice,

held twelve dynasties to a burning-glass,
laid by the sanddrifts of Cleopatra—
what were once identities simplified
to a single, indignant, collusive grin.

5

On the rainy outlook, the great shade is drawn,
my window, five feet wide, is cracked a foot,
much of the view blanked out by blind brick.
Domestic gusts of noonday Sunday cooking;
black snow grills on the fire-escape's blacker iron,
Isaiah's living coal. I too, a Sunday prophet,
hear dead sounds ascending, the fertile stench
of horsedroppings from the war-year of our birth.
Fifty-one years, how many millions gone—
this same street, West Sixty-Seven, was here then,
and this same building, the last gasp of true
Nineteenth Century Capitalistic Gothic—
horsedroppings and drippings . . . hear it, hear the clopping
of the hundreds of horses unstopping . . . each hauls a coffin.

Obit

In the end it gets us, though the man know what he'd have:
old cars, old money, old undebased pre-Lyndon
silver, no copper rubbing through . . . old wives;
I could live such a too long time with mine.
In the end, every hypochondriac is his own prophet.
Before the final coming to rest, comes the rest
of all transcendence in a mode of being, stopping
all becoming. I'm for and with myself in my otherness,
in the eternal return of earth's fairer children,
the lily, the rose, the sun on dusk and brick,
the loved, the lover, and their fear of life,
their unconquered flux, insensate oneness, their painful 'it
    was . . .'
After loving you so much, can I forget
you for eternity, and have no other choice?

Afterthought

NOTEBOOK: as my title intends, the poems in this book are written as one poem, intuitive in arrangement, but not a pile or sequence of related material. It is less an almanac than the story of my life. Many events turn up, many others of equal or greater personal reality do not. This is not my private lash, or confession, or a puritan's too literal pornographic honesty, glad to share secret embarrassment and triumph. The time is a summer, an autumn, a winter, a spring, another summer. I began working sometime in June 1967 and finished in June 1970. My plot rolls with the seasons, but one year is confused with another. I have flashbacks to what I remember, and fables inspired by impulse. Accident threw up subjects, and the plot swallowed them—famished for human chances.

I lean heavily to the rational, but am devoted to unrealism. An unrealist must not say, 'The man entered a house,' but, 'The man entered a police-whistle,' or 'Seasick with marital happiness, the wife plunges her eyes in her husband swimming like vagueness on the grass.' Or make some bent generalization: 'Weak wills command the gods.' Or more subtly, words that seem right, though loosely in touch with reason: 'Saved by my anger from cruelty.' Unrealism can degenerate into meaningless clinical hallucinations or rhetorical machinery, but the true unreal is about something, and eats from the abundance of reality.

My opening lines are as hermetic as any in the book. The 'fractions' mean that my daughter, born in January, is each July, a precision important to a child, something and a half years old. The 'Seaslug etc.' are her declining conceptions of God.

I have taken from many books, used the throwaway conversational inspirations of my friends, and much more that I idly spoke to myself. I have no wish to sleuth down my plagiarisms, but want to say that 'Hell' is taken from two paragraphs of Glenn Gray's 'The Warrior'; ideas and expressions in 'Half a Century Gone' come from Simone Weil; ideas and expressions in 'Obit' and another poem, from Herbert Marcuse. Two poems steal distortedly from the Urdu poet, Ghalib, literally translated by Aijaz Ahmad. The intelligent and not the stupid quote belongs to R. P. Blackmur in the poem dedicated to him. The borrowings from Plutarch, Sir Thomas More's son-in-law, Emerson, Coleridge, Goethe, Sir Kenneth Clark and Stonewall Jackson are easier to spot. I owe two Dante lines in 'Winter' to Philip Gambone; I also want to thank Frank Bidart for many days of help and suggestions.

My meter, fourteen line unrhymed blank verse sections, is fairly strict at first and elsewhere, but often corrupts in single lines to the freedom of prose. Even with this license, I fear I have failed to avoid the themes and gigantism of the sonnet.

A poet can be intelligent and on to what he does; yet he walks, half-balmy and over-armored—caught by his amnesia, ignorance and education. For the poet without direction, poetry is a way of not saying what he has to say. I had good guides when I began. They have gone on with me; by now the echoes are so innumerable that I almost lack the fineness of ear to distinguish them.

In truth I seem to have felt mostly the joys of living; in remembering, in recording, thanks to the gift of the Muse, it is the pain.

ROBERT LOWELL

Note to the New Edition

This text differs from the first edition in May 1969 and the second in July. About a hundred of the old poems have been changed, some noticeably. More than ninety new poems have been added. These have not been placed as a single section or epilogue. They were scattered where they caught, intended to fulflesh my poem, not sprawl into chronicle. I am loath to display a litter of variants, and hold up a still target for the critic who knows that most second thoughts, when visible, are worse thoughts. I am sorry to ask anyone to buy this poem twice. I couldn't stop writing, and have handled my published book as if it were manuscript.

R. L.

January 1970

Dates

Dates fade faster than we do. Many in the last two years are already gone; in a year or two, most of the rest will slip. I list a few that figure either directly or obliquely in my text:

THE VIETNAM WAR, 1967.

THE ARAB-ISRAELI SIX DAYS' WAR, first week in June 1967.

THE BLACK RIOTS IN NEWARK AND ELSEWHERE, July and August 1967.

CHE GUEVARA'S DEATH, October 8, 1967.

THE PENTAGON MARCH, October 21, 1967.

EUGENE MCCARTHY'S CAMPAIGN FOR THE DEMOCRATIC NOMINATION, November 1967–August 1968.

ROBERT KENNEDY'S CAMPAIGN FOR THE DEMOCRATIC NOMINATION, February 1968–June 1968.

MARTIN LUTHER KING'S MURDER, April 4, 1968.

THE COLUMBIA STUDENT DEMONSTRATIONS, April 23 into May 1968.

THE FRENCH STUDENTS' AND WORKERS' UPRISINGS, May 2 into June 1968.

ROBERT KENNEDY'S MURDER, June 5, 1968.

THE REPUBLICAN CONVENTION IN MIAMI, August 5–9, 1968.

THE RUSSIAN OCCUPATION OF CZECHOSLOVAKIA, August 21, 1968.

THE DEMONSTRATIONS AND DEMOCRATIC CONVENTION IN CHICAGO, August 25–29, 1968.

THE VIETNAM WAR, 1968, 1969, 1970, —